WABASH COUNTY
CHRONICLES

WABASH COUNTY
CHRONICLES

Raucous Quirky & Essential Tales

by

RON WOODWARD AND
GLADYS HARVEY

Charleston · London

THE
History
PRESS

Published by The History Press
Charleston, SC 29403
www.historypress.net

Back cover, top right: Painting by Homer G. Davisson. Courtesy of Wabash
Carnegie Public Library
All images courtesy of Ron Woodward.

First published 2010

Manufactured in the United States

ISBN 978.1.59629.934.4
Woodward, Ronald.
Wabash County chronicles : raucous, quirky, and essential tales / Ron Woodward and
Gladys Harvey.
p. cm.
Includes bibliographical references.
ISBN 978-1-59629-934-4
1. Wabash County (Ind.)--History--Anecdotes. 2. Wabash County (Ind.)--Biography-
-Anecdotes. 3. Wabash County (Ind.)--History, Local--Anecdotes. I. Harvey, Gladys.
II. Title.
F532.W18W67 2010
977.2'83--dc22
2010002064

Notice: The information in this book is true and complete to the best of our
knowledge. It is offered without guarantee on the part of the authors or The History
Press. The authors and The History Press disclaim all liability in connection with the
use of this book.

This book is dedicated to Gladys Dove Harvey for her tireless efforts as a librarian, educator and public-spirited citizen.

Contents

CONTENTS

CONTENTS

Part V: Business and Industry

Introduction

S itting at a table in the middle of a museum under construction seems an odd place for inspiration to occur, but some ideas will not be deterred. Amidst hammering and pounding, two retired teachers of the Wabash City Schools came up with an idea to preserve some of the old stories of Wabash County.

Wabash County history stretches over three centuries. During that time, many fascinating people have come and gone and many unusual occurrences have transpired, most having become lost to recorded history.

This book is a natural outgrowth of the authors' pursuit to preserve local history and the stories and tales that have been passed from generation to generation. Many of these stories have been gleaned from years of attending historical and genealogical meetings, working with young people and answering hundreds of inquiries. It is hoped that this collection of stories will turn back the years and help reveal the past to another generation.

Ronald L. Woodward

Part I

Historical Tales

HANGING ROCK

Hanging Rock is a prominent, ancient landmark in Wabash County. Because of its unusual character and origin, Hanging Rock was designated on May 23, 1986, as a National Registered Natural Landmark by the U.S. Department of the Interior. Since 1962, ACRES, Inc., in agreement with the Swan family, has managed the site.

Hanging Rock was created about 400 million years ago during the Silurian Period. Throughout most of this period, a shallow inland sea covered Indiana—in fact, it covered most of North America. Corals, stromatoporiods, bryzoa, crinoids and sponges, as well as other sea creatures, built numerous small mounds (biotherms) and reefs on the sea floor.

This ancient reef has undergone considerable erosion due to oceans, glaciers, streams and man. The Wabash River has effectively opened it to our view but has removed more than half of the reef. Most of the central reef core and all of the northern flank beds are missing, leaving only the southern flank.

At one time, people used the site as a public recreation site. Boats would take visitors from Wabash to Hanging Rock for a day of picnicking and recreation. Prior to that time, people travelling through the area had visited the site. One of the first historical accounts of the site was the diary of Colonel Henry Hamilton, the famous "hair buyer" of the American Revolution. He described it as a "Sugar Loaf" along the Wabash River at

Hanging Rock, jutting out over the Wabash River, has played a vital role in the natural, American Indian and Revolutionary War heritage of Wabash County.

which his advance guard spent the night. He was on his way from Detroit to retake Fort Sackville with 521 men and allies.

Today, many people use the site to fish, while others enjoy climbing to the top of this ancient reef to view the surrounding countryside. There are no retaining walls or fences at the top. People have been known to practice rappelling from its heights. A trail starting at the parking lot makes it fairly easy to reach the top.

The area is also very rich in both flora and fauna. A few of the many plants to be found are bluebells, snow trillium, columbine, bloodroot, meadow parsnips, false solomon's seal, wild leeks, wild geranium, mullein and rock sandwort. Trees include buckeye, sycamore, hackberry, maple, ash and basswood.

Hanging Rock is rich in local tradition. Early American Indians knew it as a lovers' leap. Early settlers who moved into the area were taken with its majesty and quickly settled near it. One early family had a cabin located not far from the rock. One day, the mother of the family went to a nearby spring to get a bucket of water. She left her two-year-old son in the cabin. The toddler decided to follow his mother. Somewhere along the path, the child was nabbed by a panther (early settlers called them "painters"). The mother, hearing the commotion behind her, turned to see the child being mauled by a huge cat. The mother's screams for help were heard by neighbors, who came to help. The screams also scared the panther, which grabbed the child by the scruff of the neck and dragged him off into the woods. Neighbors took up the trail and, locating the panther, were able to kill it and rescue the child. Other than a few scrapes and bruises, the child was found to be all right. Even today, people near Hanging Rock, up and down the river, claim to either hear or see a large cat. Others claim that their dogs act strangely at times as if intimidated by something.

See also the section "Local Indian Sites" for more discussion of the lovers' leap.

Nature Gone Wild

Today's news is often filled with natural disasters, such as floods, tornadoes, hurricanes or earthquakes. It is very easy for us to focus on these natural tragedies while often forgetting those that happened closer to home.

The Miami Indians, who lived in the county in 1811, experienced one of the greatest earthquakes the Midwest has ever felt. Each year, two or three quakes rock chimneys and windows in Wabash County. But the year 1811 was different. The comet of 1811 struck fear into the hearts of inhabitants and foretold of days of doom and horror to occur. One settler described the comet's passing as such: the "air grew musty and dull and though the sun was visible like a glowing ball of copper" it was like a "mournful twilight." That very night, the heavens opened up with heavy rains and wind, and then a series of tremors, felt all the way to New York, shook the entire Mississippi Valley river system. For days, the waters of all the rivers churned and boiled. The Wabash River flowed backward for two days. The epicenter was located at New Madrid near the border of Missouri, Tennessee and Illinois. New Madrid disappeared, and so much land fell that Reelfoot Lake in Tennessee was created. Some say that we are overdue for another earthquake.

Natural fires were another problem faced by American Indians. Lightning strikes created huge fires that cleared acres upon acres of trees. Early settlers called such areas "Oak Openings" or barrens. Indians used these cleared areas for their villages and fields of maize. Pioneers took over this rich, open land for their farms. The largest "Oak Opening" in the county was the area known as the Prairie, an area stretching from Richvalley to the mouth of the Mississinewa.

Around North Manchester were large "Oak Openings" that occurred in Bear Swamp, a swamp that stretched all the way over to Lake Erie. These barrens would be acre upon acre of tall, rank, coarse, strawlike sage grass, taller than a man's head. Many a person became disoriented and lost in the tall grass. Anna Geik was one such person. She was sent to bring the cows home one evening. She got lost in the tall grass in a barren close to her home and spent the night in a tree while wolves gnawed the bark off the tree trying to get at her. The fright and exposure she endured led to her death a short time later.

Wolves were so thick in the area that they endangered human life. Indian tradition has it that a lone brave hunter, returning home with a deer slung over his shoulder, had a fatal encounter with wolves in one of the many barrens. They backed him into a hollow tree, and although he defended himself with his hatchet, his strength finally failed and he was overpowered and devoured by the wolves.

Probably the strangest natural disaster was the Great Squirrel Stampede of 1834. Today, we see squirrels scampering through yards, eating forage on posts or tree limbs or dashing in front of our cars. But in 1834 it was more serious—in fact, it was threatening.

In the fall of 1834, Wabash County—in fact the entire state of Indiana—was overrun by squirrels. Early settlers equated them to an army on the move. The vast hordes were so thick that their weight would cause tree limbs to fall. They would completely denude an area of vegetation and then move on. It's hard to imagine such a horde of cute little creatures creating such devastation. The corn crop was nearly decimated. The Wabash River could not stop the little varmints. They swam the river or scampered across the overhanging tree limbs, often forming a living chain for other squirrels to cross over on.

For ten days, squirrels reigned supreme over the county, bringing devastation and ruin. Farmers defended their crops as best they could. In fact, one settler recalled how farmers kept themselves busy shooting the varmints to keep them from their crops. Kids were sent out with clubs to beat them off. After ten days, the squirrels moved on to fresher fields. No one knows what caused the squirrel stampede.

➤◆➤

KERR LOCK

The Kerr Lock at Lagro was part of the Wabash and Erie Canal, a system 380 miles long in Indiana. It had a six-foot lift and was made of cut stone. Construction on the canal began in 1832, and the last portion was abandoned in 1888. During the canal days, Lagro had numerous businesses, including seven grain elevators, two packinghouses, twenty-three saloons, a racetrack, three blacksmith shops and many warehouses and hotels. In the early days of the canal, Lagro was a thriving community. Many people traveled down the canal, sometimes getting off at a different place and remaining in the area, becoming Wabash County's early citizens.

There were four locks near Lagro, carved by German stonemasons. Locks were named for the man who opened the gate for the canalboats. Jim Kerr

Kerr Lock was built in the community of Lagro by Irish laborers as a lock on the Wabash and Erie Canal. Now it is preserved as a park for the community.

An early scene at the train depot and elevator at Lagro. Lagro was named for the Miami Indian chief LeGres. The train first arrived in 1857, replacing the canal in importance.

was one operator. Ironically, he died one night in 1885 crossing his own lock while intoxicated.

There were three kinds of boats: packet boats for passengers; line boats for freight; and canalboats for both freight and passengers.

The ropes made of hemp were attached to the animals that pulled the boats. The ropes were 150 to 250 feet long. Two to six mules or horses were used to pull a boat and were changed every ten miles. They traveled three to six miles per hour. Some animals were transported in the boats as relief animals.

Sometimes, when a low bridge was ahead, the boat master would yell out "Low Bridge!" for those on the top deck. The boatman would sound a horn to announce the arrival of a packet boat in an area, and the townspeople or people living near would hurry to get any mail, news or gossip and sometimes meet people who were stopping over.

On the packet boats, the ladies' room was located at the bow, and alongside was a cabin with a hand basin, towels, a comb and a brush. The rule was that no gentleman could visit this room unless all ladies gave permission. In the stern was the kitchen and steward's room, and in the middle was a large sitting room, used as a men's sleeping room at night. Berths of sleeping quarters were shelves of boards three feet wide, six feet long and staggered in tiers of three along either side of the room. Togetherness was obvious.

The Wabash and Erie Canal served a real purpose in early Wabash history; however, when railroads came into being, transportation of

St. Patrick's Catholic Church, built by Irish laborers from the Wabash and Erie Canal who remained in the area.

people and farm products proved to be not only much faster but also more economical. And following this period, the invention and popularity of motorized vehicles made a still greater impact on life in early Indiana and Wabash County.

The Kerr Lock was no. 14. It was built on July 31, 1834, by a Mr. Matlock. The stone came from a quarry south of Lagro near the Narrows. At least four people drowned in the lock. One was William Walker; he fell in while drunk and was found west of the lock and hauled out with boat hooks. Another was "Corky" Taylor; he drowned in 1860.

HORSE RACING IN THE CANAL

When the first section of the canal west of the Wabash Lock had been constructed in 1836, it was found that the bottom of the "ditch" was very level and smooth, and the sporting portion of the community took advantage of the same by using it for a racetrack.

The Ricketts brothers, William and John, who assisted in the construction of the lock, owned two horses that had a "record" among canal men. John had a nice bay mare, and William had a sorrel hip-shot horse, which was the fastest even though it looked slow.

While cutting stone for the Wabash Lock, William and John heard of a fast horse owned by William Armitage at Logansport, and they decided to see which was faster. They met and set a date and raced the bay mare. It lost, but John was satisfied; he was just testing the horse to see its speed.

Logansport "bloods" made a big deal over the victory and taunted Wabash unmercifully. Finally, they offered a challenge to race any horse between Logansport and east to the state line for any sum.

Ricketts saw an edge here and arranged for a $200 side bet. The race would take place in the canal bed at Wabash against the hip-shot sorrel. It turned out to be sort of a pioneer "Derby Day." A huge crowd turned out, and bets were made by everyone.

The evening before the proposed race, it rained, making the track wet and muddy. Holes had to be dug to drain off the water. By 3:00 p.m., it was partially dry. When the horses were led out, the Logansport crowd laughed and jeered when they saw Ricketts's ungainly sorrel led out.

"Go" was the stern command at the starting point. They went at a lively pace. The sorrel led by several lengths and gained rapidly. The riders urged their steeds to the utmost, yelling from the start like wild Comanches. The wire was passed with "sorrel hippy" two lengths ahead. A shout went up from the Wabash people that would have drowned out Niagara Falls.

❧

THE IRISH WAR IN WABASH COUNTY

When the Wabash and Erie Canal was built in the early 1830s in Wabash County, many Irishmen were brought in to work on the canal. They represented two groups: the Catholic Corkonians from County Cork and the Protestant Far Downs from County Down in Ireland. These two factions had worked in the Chesapeake area, did not get along there and brought their animosities with them when they came to work on the canal.

Both groups of Irishmen brought their families with them, as well as their religious differences. They lived in makeshift shanties in squalid labor camps. The camps would spring up almost overnight. Many sites are lost to history, but several were located on the outskirts of communities like Lagro and still exist today in a section referred to as Hell's Half Acre. While the men worked, the women took care of the children and prepared meals for their husbands. It was in these camps that men sought solace with their families after a twelve-hour day. Yet at night these camps often became targets for others.

Contractors had learned early on in Maryland that the Irish were of two groups and needed to be separated. The Far Downs worked below Wabash, while the Corkonians worked near Lagro. Occasionally, fights between the two groups would break out. By July 1835, the situation between the two groups had reached a breaking point. During the daytime, work on the canal was constantly interrupted when rumors circulated that one party or the other was marching to attack. At night, the families left their shanties to sleep in the woods without a fire, out of fear of being burned or murdered in their sleep. Each group was envious of the work assigned to the other group and, armed with shovels, knives, axes and whatever tools they had, approached the other faction.

The anniversary of the Battle of the Boyne, a 1690 battle fought in Ireland between the forces of William III and James II, increased the violence between these two groups. The ringleaders egged the riot on and promoted it, encouraging the two groups to fight.

In July 1835, not much work on the canal was done due to danger and fears involved, so the superintendent of construction of the canal met with one faction and then the other, trying to persuade them to work in peace. One group had organized as many as three hundred ready to fight. The battle was fought at the bottom of Wilson's Bluff, just west of Lagro near Enyeart's Creek.

People living in the area were so concerned that they sent word to Fort Wayne and also to Logansport for militia to curb the violence. Captain Elias Murray took command of the temporary garrison formed at Lagro. Colonel John Spencer led the Fort Wayne troops, and General John Tipton led the Logansport militia. With the appearance of the militia and mediation from David Burr, the riot came to an end. Nearly two hundred were arrested on both sides, and eight ringleaders were arrested and sent under armed guard to Indianapolis, where they were later released.

As a curious side note to the affair, Chief Godfroy of the Miami Indians was so appalled by the actions of the workers that he offered his services to end the war.

EARLY EDUCATION

The first term of school taught in Wabash was held during the winter of 1836–37, three short years after the founding of Wabash. Ira Burr was the first teacher, and he taught in an old deserted storage room on Lot 26 of the original plat. The building was owned by William S. Edsall. It was

A picture of an early Wabash County school classroom, taken about 1900. These classrooms replaced the log cabin schools that were first used.

followed in 1837 by a school taught by Sarah Blackman on an adjacent lot. The third school was taught in the fall and winter of 1837–38 by Emma Swift.

The first schoolhouse built and owned by the village of Wabash was a frame structure erected by Colonel Hugh Hanna in 1843. The house was a frame building eighteen by thirty feet in dimensions and was located on a little hill near the junction of Huntington and Maple Streets. The place was a very pleasant one, especially for the teacher. North of the schoolhouse was a thick grove of beech switches, which were as necessary to the education of some of the youths as their spelling books or arithmetic. On the south side was Colonel Hanna's sugar camp, where in the springtime the village suitor escorted his sweetheart to treat her to a deluge of taffy. On the other side of the building was a large field that never failed to produce a rich harvest of wheat or corn. The yard was a pleasant place for the honest children to scamper about barefooted in summer and wearing coats in winter. Warren Hanna was one of the boys who began his educational career in the old building. He was licked three times one afternoon for pinching a fellow pupil with a pair of old-fashioned tweezers. Wabash's first schoolhouse was used until 1851.

By 1872, there were rules and regulations for teachers. Some were as follows:

Teachers each day will fill lamps, clean chimneys and trim wicks.

Each teacher will bring a bucket of water and a scuttle of coal for the day's session.

Make your pens carefully; you may whittle nibs to the individual taste of pupils.

Men teachers may take one evening each week for courting purposes or two evenings a week if they go to church regularly.

After ten hours in school, the teachers spend the remaining time reading the Bible or other good books.

Women teachers who marry or engage in unseeming conduct will be dismissed.

Each teacher should lay aside from each pay, a goodly sum of his earnings for his benefit during his declining years so that he will not become a burden to society.

Any teacher who smokes, uses liquor in any form, frequents pool or public halls, or gets shaved in a barber shop will give good reason to suspect his worth, intentions, integrity and honesty.

The teacher who performs his labors faithfully and without fault for five years will be given an increase of 25 cents per week in his pay, providing the Board of Education approves.

This was early education in Wabash.

SCHOOLS OF LONG AGO

Early schools of Wabash County had many interesting local names. The county, when it built schools, assigned numbers to the school, such as District School Number 5. Local residents soon gave them more colorful names, such as Turkey Pen School, Indian School, Bussard School, Point Lookout School, Africa School and Swamp School.

An early school picture taken outside of a brick school in Wabash County. Brick township schools replaced log cabin and frame buildings beginning in the 1870s.

The early subscription schools were held in log cabins with a huge open fireplace, clay jambs and a stick and clay chimney. It wouldn't be until the 1860s and 1870s that brick would be used. The students' seats were made of split poles with legs in them. The floor and writing desks were puncheons dressed off with an axe and laid on wooden pins driven into the walls. For windows, a log on one side was left out and the space was covered with greased paper.

School was generally held during the months of December through February. It met six days a week from 6:00 a.m. to 6:00 p.m.

There were many old customs associated with these early "blab" schools. One of the oldest was the "Barring of the Master." One extreme case of this occurred in Lagro Township. School was commonly held on Christmas Day in those good ol' days. But on that day, "scholars" would come early, way before the teacher. The students would then "bar" the door so the teacher could not enter. The windows would be fastened shut. When the teacher appeared, he or she was unable to enter and would

A picture of children during school recess at Small's Settlement on Treaty Creek. During recess, children were left to their own devices, often playing various games.

stand outside yelling at them to open up. The "scholars" would hand out a piece of paper with demands on it. Generally, these demands were for a treat and the day off. If the teacher acquiesced to these demands, the door was thrown open and the teacher was allowed to enter.

Occasionally, the master refused to sign and would undertake to get in by breaking down the door or coming through the clapboard roof or down through the chimney. At such times, a general mêlée would break out with desks broken, objects thrown and more. This generally resulted in the teacher being overpowered and tied hand and foot. The "scholars" would then head for the "crick," where another offer to sign would be made. If the master again refused, he was "soused" (dunked) until he signed.

Most schoolmasters expected the barring out and went along with it, giving out apples or cookies and the day off. However, in Lagro Township on one Christmas, the demands went too far. The local "scholars" barred out the teacher and not only demanded the day off but a gallon whiskey as well. The teacher signed off but struck out the whiskey. This they did not notice and let him in. Presently, one of the older boys discovered the change. He gathered the rest of the scholars and they "tossed him out."

The master, not to be outdone, climbed onto the roof and placed a board over the chimney. The smoke filled the schoolhouse and drove the "scholars" out. As they came out, the rod was liberally applied to the seat of their britches, and they spent the rest of the day in class.

WABASH COUNTY HOME

Wabash County care for the poor evolved slowly. Originally, Wabash County had a position called overseer of the poor. Two such overseers were appointed for each township by the county commissioners. They were responsible for the care of the poor within the county. They were able to bind out or farm out poor who were unable to care for themselves and helped them with medical care. They were to keep records of those who were unable to care for themselves and needed relief. They were further authorized to apprentice all poor children whose parents were either dead or unable to support them. Males were to be bound out until age twenty-one and females until age eighteen. They could also farm out or indenture all poor persons who became a public charge.

At the first meeting of the county commissioners in June 1835, J. Galahan and A.H. Keller were appointed as overseers for Lagro Township and Hugh Hanna and David Burr for Noble Township. The system became cumbersome and was replaced when the county established a Wabash County Home for the purpose of seeing after the needs of the poor. In September 1849, the county commissioners bought a farm "for the purpose of supporting the poor of the county," paying $16 per acre, totaling $3,000. Land was purchased from George E. Gordon located at the present-day southeast corner of the intersection of State Road 13 and U.S. 24, Section 36, Township 28N, Range 7E.

The County Farm was built in 1850 and since that time has been referred to as the Poor Farm, County Asylum, County Infirmary and County Farm. The home was built at a cost of $4,547.93. The first superintendent was George W. Sailors, who was paid $125.00 a year. Later superintendents who we know about were James Gamble, Henry Olin, Jeremiah Judd

(1851), James McFarland (1852–54), James Johnson (1857), George A. Wellman, John Enyeart, Ezekiel P. Lowry (1860), D. Reniker (1864), John L. Gamble, William Asher Gray (1868–70), William A. Richards (1875–85), Joseph H. Bantham (1894–1902), Erwin Thompson, D.M. Hubbard (1914–18), James Gamble (1922–24), William Curless (1953–57) and Melvin Anderson (1966–74).

Superintendents lived with their families at the County Farm. They were also able to hire farmhands to help keep the place running. It was hoped that the residents would raise their own truck crops and necessary farm animals. It was, to a degree, self-supporting. Residents would help with various projects and duties around the place. An orchard was planted and maintained by the residents.

In 1851, $1,345.47 was paid out by the county commissioners for the care of the poor during the year ending May 31. The commissioners accepted sealed proposals from local doctors for the rendering of medical services and medicine for one year to the paupers at the County Farm. In 1857, the county commissioners passed an order requiring the superintendent, James Johnson, to make the paupers work as many hours each day as a "physician shall say they are able to work." In 1859, a well was dug and walled for the use of the residents.

By 1860, the County Farm was kept by Ezekiel P. Lowry and had eight residents: Bethanie Flint, Laura Kendall, Patrick Kerney, Ann Murphy, Edwin Murphy, Peter O'Rorke, Edward Paco and Michael Tumy. The youngest was thirteen and the oldest sixty-six.

In April 1865, the County Farm burned to the ground. The fire originated in a defective flue. It was decided that it would be rebuilt "as it is a paying concern." In September 1867, the county commissioners visited the County Farm and found everything in good condition.

In March 1869, the commissioners reported that during the last year twenty-two people had been received at the County Farm, twenty-one had died and twelve were then in residence.

In 1870, Asher Gray reported there were eighteen residents. The youngest was born in February of that year, and the oldest was 106.

In 1876, William Richards reported forty-three residents. By the end of the year, there were thirty-nine residents—sixteen females and twenty-three males.

In 1880, William Richards reported forty-eight residents—the youngest, eleven months old, and the oldest, seventy-nine.

By 1885, several grand jury investigations had reported bad conditions for the children who were kept there. The women of the Women's Christian Temperance Union in both North Manchester and Wabash began to work for an orphanage that could better care for children. They were able to convince the county commissioners of this, and an orphanage was established in south Wabash.

In 1900, Joseph Bantham stated that there were thirty-eight residents—the youngest was thirty-two and the oldest, eighty-six.

In 1920, there were twenty-three inmates ranging from twenty-six to ninety. In 1922, the home needed repairs, and the residents were moved to the old Park Hospital until the repairs were finished.

In 1942, the County Council appropriated $5,000 from the general revenue for the construction of a new barn at County Farm.

Melvin Anderson was the last superintendent of the Wabash County Home. He and his family lived in the home and managed the farm from 1966 to 1974. It was a twenty-four-hour, seven-day-a-week job for the family. They had five rooms for themselves. His wife, Dorothy, did all the required "bookwork," such as making out the budget and menus for the month ahead. Being a county agency, every penny had to be approved and accounted for. They had four paid assistants, two cooks, a laundry woman and a cleaning lady.

Residents had private rooms furnished as they saw fit. Most had a single bed, a dresser, a TV and a rocking chair. Downstairs there was a communal recreation area that they would all share. One woman interviewed who had

Wabash County Home was begun in 1853 as a way to care for the poor and indigent of the county. It was closed by county commissioners in 1975.

been there forty-six years said, "I like the place. It is so pretty and nice. I hate to leave."

Food from the garden included sweet corn, green beans, onions, lettuce, sweet potatoes, strawberries and eggs from chickens, and animals were raised and butchered by the residents. Mrs. Anderson was able to help freeze various food items but was not permitted to can food. Meals were served family style and no food was wasted. The home underwent inspection from time to time.

Each year, the residents raised and sold canna bulbs, which proliferated on the grounds; the profits were used for a trip to town or a treat of some kind.

Residents ranged in age from thirty-nine to ninety-seven. If they could, they paid a monthly payment or relatives paid for them. If they couldn't, then the county paid part of the expenses. At the time of closing, each resident had a social security number. Mr. Anderson cut the men's hair, and the women went to the Heartland Cosmetology classes for hair care.

At Christmastime, there were various parties for the residents. The Elks Club always provided something for individuals; other groups also helped in a variety of ways. Funeral homes in Wabash would sometimes bring out baskets of flowers left over from funerals.

Wabash County commissioners Glen Berry, Clarence Bowman and Eugene Schenkel closed the County Home in October 1974.

AFTER THE CANALS CAME THE TRAINS

In 1856, the first passenger train arrived in Wabash over the Toledo, Wabash and Western Railroad. That was a great day for Wabash citizens. Generally, it also meant the beginning of the demise of the canal system. The impact that railroads had on the public meant that for the first time man could travel faster than a horse and go around or through mountains. For almost a century, trains had a monopoly on transportation for people and freight.

In 1854, the *Wabash Gazette* reported that four boatloads of iron for the railroads had been received from Toledo for the Lake Erie, Wabash and

St. Louis Railroad. This meant the start of that railroad through Wabash. Soon a passenger station was built, and by 1872 a freight station was in operation. The creation of the telegraph came about via the influence of the railroad.

The history of the Big Four was also important in affecting Wabash by connecting the town with other prominent commercial centers of the Midwest and East. During the early 1900s, the Big Four was consolidated to become a part of the New York Central System of railroads.

Another railroad serving Wabash County was the Goshen, Kosciusko and Peru Railroad Company, later termed the Warsaw, Goshen and White Pigeon Railroad Company, serving the Michigan Line. It was incorporated by 1869 as the Cincinnati, Wabash and Michigan Railroad. This was a boon to the North Manchester area. Shops were located in 1872 in the eastern part of Wabash with the original passenger station located on the southwestern corner of Huntington and Canal Streets. It was later moved to East Market Street. The Big Four discontinued passenger service in 1943, hauling freight from that date on. The Vandalia route in 1852 traversed the northern part of the county. Originally, it was known as the Logansport and Northern Railroad.

Without a doubt, railroads have made an impact on Wabash and still do. With the railroads came the commercial aspect of transportation. The commercial traveler also used the trains for their purposes. Coal-burning locomotives pulled local trains made up of mail cars, baggage cars, smoking cars, dining cars and coaches. In the old coaches, reversible red plush seats were worn shiny. With no air conditioning in the early coaches, windows were open and cinders would fly about.

The early Pullman ride was a thrilling experience. Going to bed on a Pullman car meant a routine: placing your shoes in the aisle outside to be shined; visiting a crowded restroom; sleeping in a hammock, a so-called bed—all with the trains lurching back and forth. Meals on a Pullman were generally served from a small kitchen and by waiters balancing trays of food. You never filled your coffee cup to the brim, as a sudden lurch meant disaster. Porters were often called "George," probably after George W. Pullman of the Pullman Company. For many years, the train depot was a meeting place for friends parting as well as arriving.

A famous train that passed through Indiana was the 1865 Lincoln funeral train, cars draped in black, as it went from Springfield, Illinois, to Washington, D.C. It was an empty train, but it was an event Wabash citizens did not forget.

Mergers of the railroad corporations and ownerships have made numerous changes in the names of railroads. Today, travel by train is becoming uncommon. The Norfolk and Western may have been the last passenger train through Wabash. A last run was used as an excursion for children to go from Wabash to Peru—affording schoolchildren the experience of riding on a train.

Today, Wabash sees many trains traveling through the town, most not stopping. They carry freight from automobiles to chemicals. The railroads have served the community in the past and present, making for an effective form of transportation.

RIDING THE RAILS

The sound of the iron horse has incited wanderlust since the nation's first railroad tracks were laid more than a century and a half ago. The sound of that train whistle in the distance sparks an element of intrigue. And that produced the hobo, a well-known element of our past society.

A hobo is defined as a traveling or itinerant laborer or perhaps craftsman—someone who lived life on the move, usually riding the trains. He sometimes worked for food, lodging or even clothing. Wabash has had its share of hobos at various times.

Hoboing used to be a way of life. There was even a national organization of sorts that held hobo conventions and elected a "King of Tramps." Members had their own Morse code of sorts, a code of symbols to guide others along the way. These chalk symbols scrawled on fences, walls, gateposts and other places told a fellow hobo whether a community or house was good or bad. Such symbols indicated a host of attributes: good for a handout, a cranky woman, a bad dog, food for work, a clean jail, hostile police, keep away, a woman alone, poor people, a spot to sleep in a loft, a kind woman, sit-down food, sanctimony, a cop lives there, bad prospects, good prospects, the clink is certain, a sob story will pay off, take this road and good for clothes.

These signs could be posted on gateposts, in depots or in hobo jungles. During the Depression years, hoboing was very popular. However, the days after the Civil War truly gave birth to those unable to resist the whistle's call.

Today it is a lifestyle. On the rails, it is easier to distance oneself from one's past. Hobos sometimes have been called the "black sheep" of the family.

Railroad jungles were hobo-made shelters located near the railroad tracks, often under bridges or in tree-covered areas. Hobos built open fires with whatever they could find, from wood to paper. They warmed themselves by the fire, made mulligan stew from vegetables they had begged and heated beans and prepared coffee in three-pound coffee cans. They drank the coffee right out of the tin can and then rested and visited with one another until ready to move on.

Few hobos gave their given names, but all had a popular nickname, such as the St. Louis Kid, Jersey Slim, Philadelphia Ike and the like. One hobo familiar to Wabash was Ray "Alabam" Green. He worked for years at the Rock City Restaurant. He rode the rails for decades beginning in 1921 but stopped in the 1960s. Every summer, he used to return to Wabash to visit.

Authors have explained the difference between hobos, tramps and bums. A hobo is someone who rides the trains and is willing to work; he will chop wood, paint, weed gardens or do whatever the housewife may ask him to do. A tramp doesn't ride the rails; he walks—as in *tramp, tramp, tramp*—or he hitches rides, but he may work for food. Bums don't work; they beg and they usually stay in one place.

People tend to look at hoboing as romantic, but it's not safe. There have been many accidents involving hobos. Today, closed railroad cars make it difficult to get a ride, and train personnel and police are always on the lookout for hobos catching rides. A person today is likely to get into hoboing to see what's beyond the bend in the road, so wanderlust is the big factor. And most people become hobos before the age of thirty years and before having a career, marriage and children.

There have been hobos not commonly recognized as such. Charlie Chaplin was a real hobo at one time. Einstein was one of the best friends of hobos in the New Jersey area. He lived near Hoboken, New Jersey, which is thought to be the origin of the word "hobo." Jack London was saved from the hobo life by an older hobo. Red Skelton popularized the name "Freddie the Freeloader." Other notable hobos have been United States Supreme Court justice William O. Douglas and entertainers Burl Ives and Art Linkletter.

Wabash hasn't always been friendly to hobos. In 1901, boys shooting a BB gun in the city park managed to put out an eye of one hobo camped out at the Hobo Cave. The Hobo Cave was an extremely large culvert located in a ravine just above the lower baseball diamond.

Known locally as the Hobo Cave, this area is located in the city park behind what used to be called General Tire. From time to time people have camped out here.

A short time later, a hobo felt the not-so-kind wrath of Officer Coppock. Coppock found the hobo intoxicated in front of Bradley Brothers Drug Store. He told the hobo to make himself scarce. He later spotted him again, at which time the hobo began running down Market Street with Coppock in hot pursuit. He caught up with him at the Big Four yards. The hobo promised again to leave. As Coppock turned to leave, the hobo became verbally abusive and began to run. Coppock again pursued him, catching him at the Big Four Bridge. Coppock found a heavy hickory switch and applied some rather heavy blows to his backside, rather vigorously.

According to a *Plain Dealer* article in January 1916, "So far there have been only 138 hobos given shelter for the night in Wabash. This contrasts to the 212 for the same period in 1915." Today, the trains run so fast through Wabash that numbers can hardly be counted, but somewhere in their cars there are likely those who succumbed to the wanderlust a train provides. The whistle that the train engineer blows still has a haunting sound and may entice certain individuals to become hobos.

A professional hobo, known only as the Pennsylvania Kid, once returned to Wabash after a ten-year hiatus. He sauntered around town carrying a huge backpack containing all his worldly goods. He took to the road in 1928 and never left it. He always found Wabash to be a good town for hobos.

He reported, "We used to jungle up down by the river. As we were all friends and we'd meet each other in the jungle, cook up some foods, get washed up and straighten out for a while."

The Pennsylvania Kid traveled around a lot, working odd jobs on the farm, the highways and railroads. He said, "A lot of people wanted me to stay around awhile. I was a clean-cut kid, but I was in a hurry to get somewhere…Wherever you go, you always make friends. You meet people and they help you out. I never did want to settle down. But lately I think it would be the thing to do. I can't take it any more. I'll probably settle on the West Coast—maybe around Frisco where I usually hang out."

The hobo was a part of Wabash history.

<hr>

NEED FOR AN ORPHANS HOME

In the early days of Wabash County, orphan children were either indentured or left at the County Home. By 1885, public concern was directed toward better treatment for them.

In March 1885, members of the Women's Christian Temperance Union of North Manchester and Wabash joined forces to persuade the county commissioners to establish an orphans home. On March 9, the commissioners issued an order for the establishment of a home and the removal of children from the County Home to it.

On March 19, 1885, articles for the Wabash County Orphans Home Association were filed in the county auditor's office. The purpose of this organization was to provide for the care, education and support of children who had lost one or both parents. The members of the board of directors for the association were Mrs. Esta Walters, Mrs. L.B. Munson, Mrs. Ella Rhodes, Mrs. Ida R. Benham, Mrs, Lizzie Ebbinghouse, Mrs. E.S. Ross, Mrs. John Wharton, Charles Little and Clarence Stephenson.

The Water Cure/Female Seminary/Friends Academy located on Vernon and Pike Streets was secured for use as an orphanage. The

Today known as the Women's Clubhouse, this building was constructed to replace the south side orphanage, which had been destroyed by fire. After the orphanage closed, this building was used as the city hospital.

building was rented for $120.00 a year. The county agreed to pay $0.25 per child per day.

The women of the county worked to raise funds and clean up the facility. At first, expenses for the home were met by subscription, but later ice cream socials and lawn festivals were held to raise funds. By April 26, 1885, the home was ready for opening. Maria Burke was the matron in charge. The first young people to occupy the home were Martin V. Rogers, Clifford Tharp, Araminthe Denning, Benjamin Dunfee, Delmar Austin, Dora Miller, Anna Slage and George H. Davis.

At its peak, fifty-one children were in the home at one time. From its opening until the orphanage was destroyed by fire on July 20, 1888, ninety children were assisted by the home. The fire completely destroyed the orphanage.

Almost immediately, thoughts were turned to another orphanage. The new home was built by the Hipskind brothers on four lots purchased from the agricultural society at a cost of $7,548. Architects Crain and Koutsch of Logansport had received the bids for the design. The building was ready for occupation in August 1891 on West Hill Street.

When first built, it contained bathrooms (water closets), a laundry and a fruit cellar in the basement. On the first floor was a library, a reception room, a parlor, a playroom, a kitchen and a dining room. In the dining room were four tables, each seating twelve to fourteen children. At the time of the opening there were forty-seven children. On the second floor were sleeping rooms, a nursery and the matron's apartment. Mrs. Ora Jones was the first matron. All their beds were made of iron and had spring mattresses. There were as many as four children in some families, such as the Youst and Faidly families, listed that first year.

Some of the bills kept in the museum show Drs. Smith and Blount and other doctors prescribing camphor, cough mixture, castor oil, glycerin and quinine syrup. And there are also orders for readers, slates and arithmetic, geography and copy books. Based on the Act of the General Assembly, the articles of the association of the Wabash County Orphans Home stated that children under the age of thirteen who had been deprived of parental care by death of either mother or father, or both, were eligible.

On March 5, 1903, the Orphans Home was closed. The county determined that it was cheaper to send orphans to Whites Institute—thus the building was no longer used for an orphanage.

During the eighteen years of the existence of the Orphans Home, both on the south side of town and in the building on West Hill Street, records show that 169 children were placed in permanent homes, 102 were returned to their parents, 4 were legally adopted, 7 were sent to the Plainfield Reformatory, 6 were sent to the "feebleminded home" at Fort Wayne, 2 were sent to Knightstown, 2 were sent to the Hadley Home, 23 were sent to Whites Institute and 2 were sent to the Industrial School in Indianapolis. Six deaths occurred during that time.

Other matrons serving the Orphans Home on Hill Street have included Mrs. Thatcher, Mrs. Waring, Mrs. Horner, Mrs. Fanning, Mrs. Jones-Baldwin, Mrs. Hall and Mrs. Sutherland. When the home closed, the $2,297.16 left in the treasury was earmarked to be used for the care of orphans in the new hospital.

FOLLOW THE DRINKIN' GOURD

In the days leading up to the American Civil War, there were a number of Wabash citizens known to be abolitionists. Many were centered in Liberty, Lagro and Chester Townships. The heart of this local abolitionism was in the small settlement called Hicksite, now known as Lincolnville. Many of the people in that area were Hicksite Quakers and strongly believed in freedom for slaves, and they were willing to help escaped slaves. The way they helped was to form a link on the Underground Railroad.

The Underground Railroad in Wabash County started at Lafontaine, made its way to Hicksite (Lincolnville), north to Lagro, on to New Madison and through North Manchester. Names connected to this illicit system were McKimmey, Sayre and Place. However, the most prominent of the conductors in Wabash County was Martin McFarland. McFarland lived in the Lincolnville area and was described as an "ardent abolitionist with great physical courage." Once an escaping slave had reached McFarland's station, he could congratulate himself on the fact that he was then in the hands of a friend. It is said that McFarland helped hundreds of slaves fleeing to Canada. The exact number, however, we will never know. McFarland would often travel forty miles northward in transporting runaway slaves.

His method of helping slaves to escape was a large covered wagon that he had designed himself. The bed of the wagon was built expressly for the purpose of hiding the refugees. It was supplied with a false bottom, and in this secret compartment could be concealed up to a dozen fugitives. Starting at midnight, he would begin his journey with his precious cargo. He would stop at a nursery, buy up evergreens and fruit trees and pretend to be a peddler of trees. Many a time this helped him to get through the county undetected. This disguise did not always work.

One time he narrowly escaped detection and arrest, but his strong nerve and quick thinking got him through. He had gotten a later start than usual, and some of the Democrats in the area he went through were becoming suspicious of why he made so many trips. He had traveled just a short distance between Lincolnville and Lagro when a runner overtook him and warned that a group of slave catchers was looking for him and would be upon him in a few minutes. On either side of him was a dense wood; he quickly halted and ordered the eight slaves in the wagon to hide in the woods until he returned.

The fugitives, trembling "like in the grip of the Wabash shakes," quickly obeyed. McFarland continued on down the road and was soon overtaken by the slave catchers. They ordered him to halt and not only asked questions but also searched the wagon. McFarland denied any knowledge of slaves and stuck to his story of peddling fruit trees. Although suspicious of him, they let him go. He returned, got the slaves and proceeded on his way.

In another instance, McFarland was able to keep a slave on his property for several months before she made her escape to Canada. It seems that McFarland's neighbors woke up one day to a new neighbor in their midst. An attractive and apparently highly accomplished young lady was living with the McFarland family. At once, there was a streak of curiosity among the neighborhood as to who she was and what she was doing there, particularly among the young men of the community. The young lady was introduced as the daughter of an old friend of McFarland's in Ohio. She was anxious to obtain a school in the neighborhood, and if she could, she would remain for the winter.

Wherever this young lady went, she left a favorable impression. She had a sunny disposition and easy and accomplished manners and charm; she won over the whole community. There was a spirited rivalry among the young men for the honor of acting as her escort at the numerous apple cuttings, quilting bees and other social amusements of that day.

A young man by the name of Horace Smith was very assiduous in his attentions to her. It was soon whispered that Horace was desperately in love with her. As quickly as she had appeared, though, so too did she disappear. Many, including Horace, asked what had happened to her. McFarland told everyone that her father had become sick and that she had to return home. About three weeks later, Horace received a letter postmarked Windsor, Canada. It read:

> *Mr. Horace Smith: Kind Friend. No doubt this letter will give you a great surprise. The Miss whom you made so happy by your kindly and gentlemanly attentions during her brief stay at that good man, Mr. McFarland, was only a poor slave, making her way to a land in which she could breathe the air of freedom. Pardon me for the deception I practiced upon you, as it was impossible for me to disclose my real character to you. Hoping that your entire life may be as happy as you made mine during my stay at Mr. McFarland's.*

Neither he nor the community could believe that the young lady, whom they had come to love so well, was a Negro slave. Her father had been a rich plantation owner who had fallen on bad times and had to sell her with his other property.

Fiddle Contests

Bring your fiddles, your jew's-harps, your pennywhistles…and make music to entertain Wabash. At the 1906 Old Settlers Day in Wabash, much merriment came from the Old Fiddlers Contest. Individuals Felix Fougeres, William Brown, William Patterson, Frank Owen and Jerome Wellman—all contestants—caused the park to shake with applause. Judges for the fiddler contest were J.H. Lefforge, Dr. P.G. Moore and S.J. Payne. Winners were William Patterson (first), Felix Fougeres (second) and William Brown (third). This was just one example of fiddlers' contests in Wabash. It was a great day to be entertained by fiddlers in the community.

Fiddle contests in the United States appeared as early as 1736. Sometimes fiddle contests were just social gatherings but became contests that grew into popular annual affairs. Even as late as 1926, Henry Ford, who was greatly interested in old-time fiddling, held contests at his Ford dealership.

Old-time fiddlers used to keep a rattlesnake tail inside the fiddle. They thought it improved the tone, prevented mice from attacking the instrument and collected dust inside the instrument.

As a pioneer violinist, Johnny Hamilton's fame will not die out as long as there lives a single old-timer to relate his remarkable feats with the bow and fiddle. He was the music teacher in the pioneer days in eastern Wabash County. He gave instructions to all who came his way to learn the mysteries of the catgut music. If there was a log rollin', corn shuckin', wood choppin' or play party of any kind for miles around, he did not fail to entertain!

Some fiddle classics included "Old Dan Tucker," "Old Joe Clark," "Chicken Reel," "Handsome Molly," "Black-Eyed Susie," "Dixie," "Cotton-Eyed Joe," "Spanish Two Step," "Oh, Them Golden Slippers," "Red Wing" and "Cripple Creek." Other old tunes often played included "The Keys of

Canterbury" and "Paper of Pins," both English game songs. "A Young May Who Wouldn't Hoe Corn" and "Hog Drovers" were play party songs. Also played were "Lazy John," "Shady Grove," "The Millers Song," "The Girl on the Greenbriar Shore," "Darling Cory" and "White Cockade."

An early traveler through Wabash County attended a dance held in the "interior of a log-house, about sixteen feet by twenty…The air was hot almost to suffocation, but the site was at times too pretty, at times too comic to be quickly deserted." He found most of the girls "beating time with their little feet in jigs, reels and hornpipes." He was fascinated by the fiddler, the only musician in action who played from one tune to another "abruptly from the wildest allegro to the most dolorous of the dolefuls." The fiddler complained that he had received only two bottles of whiskey for his performance and had drunk both, but his throat was still dry. "He looked wildly around, began to cry and fell sobbing." The male dancers seized him by the arms and legs and carried him out into the yard. The dancing had ceased, but one of the party offered to find a sober fiddler. While they were looking for a fiddler, a young man began making music by bending "his knees a little and began slapping them in time with the palms of his hands." Another fiddler was found and the dance continued. "A little after twelve…the second fiddler was carried out and laid on the grass, while a third was soon found to take his place."

There were many other musical instruments popular with our pioneers. Some, such as spoons or bones, became rhythm instruments to accompany any group. In fact, the so-called spoons could be made of any household item. When they were made of flat pieces of wood, they were also called "clappers." And even washboards were used as music-making material.

The bass sound in music could come from blowing across the top of a jug. Jug bands were found even in the early 1930s and were sometimes labeled as the "poor man's tuba." Jug music was generally traced to itinerant Louisville players. Any size jug or bottle could be used; the larger the container, the deeper the sound.

Since Wabash County had an influx of Irish people during the canal days, the tin whistle became a musical instrument often associated with poor Irish. Some whistles were called pennywhistles and when blown could range in sound from very happy to quite sad. Some whistles were also carved from wood as well as made from tin.

Still another popular music maker was the jew's-harp or jaw harp. Known by different names worldwide, it is a small vibrating harp-like metal item, and when held against the teeth or lip and plucked with the fingers it produces a vibrant sound. Although credited in England as early as the 1500s, the jew's-harp was reported in the United States as an item used in payment for a tract of Indian land and used in barter with Indians. Some were considered as toys for children.

An American folk musical instrument that likely had its roots in the Appalachian Mountains was the musical saw. A unique sound was created by bending a hand saw blade and moving a fiddle bow across the saw. The saw blade was held firmly between the knees. It caught on as "mountain music," but by the 1920s and '30s it had become associated with vaudeville entertainment. Later, renowned composers even wrote compositions and solos just for the saw. Today, the sound of the saw is still heard primarily in bluegrass and country western music.

Introduced in North America by 1862, the harmonica—a reed instrument at first about four inches in diameter with steel reeds arranged together in small channels—became a popular musical instrument and is still used today. When blown by the lips, it produced harmonies of several tones. It changed in style from a small four-inch form to one much longer. Various modifications made it popular even in today's musical world. Over ninety different models of the harmonica are known today.

The five-string banjo descended from the three-string West African gourd instrument brought to America by slaves. It was known early as a "merry wang" and also as a bajor or bajar.

In 1899, a Wabash mandolin club entertained in concerts. The "potato bug" mandolin originated from the lute. This mandolin was rounded, had a lute-like back and was constructed of alternating strips of light and dark wood that made it look like a potato bug.

Still another Appalachian influence on the Wabash musical scene was the dulcimer, also known as the zither. The dulcimer was used for musical entertainment and for playing hymns at devotion time. In the early twentieth century, with the popularity of guitars and banjos, the dulcimer faded in use. But by the early 1950s, a resurgence of sorts had revived the dulcimer with urban folk music based on its nostalgic, sweet sound; it is often used as a solo instrument. Of course, the banjo, an American invention, and the guitar have become widely used in the musical world.

Wabash musical entertainment took many forms, and contests became popular with the citizens of early times. Many other instruments came into popular use with the influence of different immigrant cultures. However, from the fiddle to the tin whistle to the jew's-harp and musical saw, music definitely became a part of early Wabash life.

———◆———

LIFE AT CAMP WABASH

In 1862, Wabash life was interrupted by the American Civil War. Wabash County had already sent men into action in the Eighth Indiana Regiment. It was now being called upon for even more sacrifice. The following is a composite account of what life was like for a young man about to enter Camp Wabash and the Civil War.

July 17, 1862: John U. Pettit has been appointed post commandant to organize the regiment to be raised in this Congressional District, which will rendezvous at Wabash. Mr. Pettit has received his instructions and proceeded to perform his duties.

"Where will be the camp of the regiment to be organized here?" is a question I hear asked frequently and one that we are unable to answer. It will doubtless be near some good spring of water, on high and dry ground—where there is shade and shelter and space enough for regimental drill.

July 24, 1862: A full company for the Seventy-fifth Regiment has already been raised in Hamilton County, and our informant thinks that another company will be full in eight or ten days. Hurrah for old Hamilton! A company from Grant County is ready to go into camp whenever the word shall be given. If Grant and Hamilton don't hurry up, Wabash, I don't know what will.

Samuel Steele has been commissioned a second lieutenant and authorized to raise a company for the Seventy-fifth. Steele, Harry Wheeler and William H. Wilson are actively engaged in recruiting. Already they have enough to go into camp and will do so as soon as the camp is ready. This is quick work, for the boys only got ready last Saturday. They will have a full company by the last of next week.

The camp of the Seventy-fifth has been located in a beautiful grove, just across the river, and near the fine spring at the old stone quarry. The parade ground will be in the field above the camp, on the farm of Allen W. Smith. This camp will be one of the finest in the state. The spring, the grove and the river will make it all that can be desired. Pure, wholesome spring water for drinking and cooking, a delightful grove for shade and the river for bathing are a rare combination.

Calvin Cowgill has been appointed quartermaster, and Captain William O'Brian, of Noblesville, adjutant, of the Seventy-fifth. Both are considered excellent appointments. Everybody who knows Cowgill is sure that under his management all will be well fed, clothed and provided with everything the law allows. Captain O'Brian has seen action with the Sixteenth and knows all about organizing and drilling the men. Besides, he is a perfect gentleman and a clever fellow.

July 31, 1862: Captain Steele's company is the first company reported full in the state, and his commission was the first one issued to any officer. Six companies for the Seventy-fifth have already reported and been accepted. In addition to those we have named elsewhere, there is one from Huntington, Captain Gosshorn, one from Jay County and one from Howard. Other companies are forming sufficiently to fill the regiment.

Dr. Sprague, at North Manchester, is engaged in enlisting volunteers for a second company from Wabash County. On Monday last, he had forty-five names on his muster roll. The company will soon be filled up. From the present appearances, there will be no drafting in this county!

In five days eighty-four men enlisted from this county. They assembled at the courthouse last Friday and elected the following officers: Samuel Steele, captain, Harry Wheeler, first lieutenant, W.H. Wilson, second lieutenant.

Captain Steele went to Indianapolis the following day and obtained their commissions. In the meantime recruiting has continued and they lack but four or five of having a full company.

Captain Isaac H. Montgomery filed with Adjutant General Noble, on Monday, the roll of a company raised in Tipton County for the Seventy-fifth showed an enrollment and muster of eighty-seven men. The following officers were commissioned for this company: Isaac H. Montgomery, captain, G.L. Shaw, first lieutenant, and Noah W. Parker, second lieutenant. Well done for Tipton. Let traitors tremble!

We said last week, "Hurrah for old Hamilton," and we repeat it. Last Tuesday evening we were surprised to see a full company get off the train, form ranks and, with flag flying and drums beating, march downtown to headquarters at the town pump. They deposited the carpet-sacks and got water. They were the company of Captain McCole from Noblesville, ready to go into camp. The boys brought nothing with them but their carpet-sacks and a few canteens. They expected to find tents and camp gear here ready for them but were soon disappointed. However, they found comfortable quarters at the hotels and among the local citizens and will continue to do so until the camp is ready. The company numbers 116 and their officers are Captain C.J. McCole, First Lieutenant John H. Butler and Second Lieutenant John Bauchert. When the boys left Noblesville another company was forming and had 55 on their rolls. They expected to fill up the company this week.

August 7, 1862: The Hamilton, Madison and Jay County companies arrived here last week before the quartermaster's stores were received, and it was necessary for the men to find temporary quarters. For this purpose, the fairground west of town was found to be the best place. Its shade and booths afforded shelter from the weather. Its grounds afforded a fine place for drilling. A sufficient quantity of straw was hauled in for bedding. A cooking stove was taken out to make coffee, and arrangements were made with Messieurs Huffman, Ditton and Egnew to furnish bread, while Mr. Ditton cooked the meats and vegetables and conveyed them out to the grounds. Blankets, comforts, quilts and tableware were obtained from the citizens. Mr. Egnew took out a small grocery, and the men had a merry time of it until the storm came up on Monday night when we got well soaked. The next day they skedaddled over the river, where they found more comfortable quarters in their tents.

No name has yet been given to the camp. We suggest that it be called Camp Pettit in honor of the commandant, Colonel Pettit!

Holt and Burdge have the contract for supplying the Seventy-fifth with flour and meal while it remains in Camp Pettit. Ruddle & Sons furnish the fresh meats.

The company from Madison County is officered by Captain Joseph F. Smith, First Lieutenant Frazier, Second Lieutenant William Fillpot. They came into camp with sixty men. There are enough men already enlisted in Madison County, but we learn that they have not yet been able to unite upon satisfactory terms with Captain Smith.

There was preaching at the camp on Sunday morning and at five o'clock in the evening. Elder Miller of the ME Church preached to a very large group of people. The elder made a short but thrilling address to the soldiers. The services were conducted in an orderly manner and produced a fine impression on all.

The officers of the Jay County company are Captain C.S. Arthur, First Lieutenant Stanten and Second Lieutenant A.C. Rush. The company arrived here last Saturday and took up temporary quarters with the Noblesville boys at the fairground.

The camp of the Seventy-fifth was opened by Captain Steele's company on Monday. The boys got their tents and camp equipments and broke ground in the afternoon. They were thoroughly initiated into the mysteries and perils of camp life during the storm of Monday night. None of the tents was upset but the boys got completely soaked. Fortunately, no trees were blown down in the campground, and none of the men was injured. They all reported able for breakfast on Tuesday morning.

Since then, Captain McCole's, Captain Smith's and Captain Arthur's companies, as well as Captain Wall's company from Huntington and Captain Bryant's from Kokomo, have gone into camp. The men are enthusiastic in praise of the ground selected for the camp. They are delighted with the surroundings.

Other companies are expected daily, and the Seventy-fifth will soon be organized, armed and equipped ready for duty. None of the regimental officers for the Seventy-fifth has been appointed yet, except Assistant Surgeon Dr. White. The Seventy-fifth has been under marching orders ever since last Saturday. We will wake up some morning and leave.

At least 1,100 men are now in camp. This does not include Captain Stretch's cavalry of 150 men, who are quartered all over town, nor Captain Stone's company of 108 men, who have dispersed to their homes.

The commissioned officers met Tuesday night and recommended the following as regimental officers: John U. Pettit for colonel; William O'Brian, lieutenant colonel; McCole Major, captain; and Lieutenant Gosshorn as quartermaster.

Sunday was a great day in camp. Everybody, including women and children, was there. The people of town and surrounding countryside were there. The crowd was about three thousand. Reverend H.S. Skinner preached in the morning and Elder Shortridge of Valparaiso in the evening. The majority of the soldiers behaved themselves in a very orderly manner, but there were many wild and reckless boys among them.

August 21, 1862: Last Sunday night a messenger from the governor arrived by special train, with an order for the Seventy-fifth to proceed immediately to Indianapolis. Early Monday morning, everything was in motion. Tents were struck, camp equipage and baggage packed and all hauled to the depot. The railroad company refusing to furnish, on such short notice, a sufficient number of cars to transport the troops, Colonel Pettit ordered over from the camp two companies of troops and took military possession of the road. In short time, he had four or five trains of empty cars at the depot. At 2:00 p.m., the regiment got aboard and bade the town farewell. A large crowd assembled at the depot to bid the men goodbye. We went off cheering lustily and arrived at Indianapolis without accident.

⤙◈⤚

From One-Horse Plows to Diesel Farming

Farming has generally been known as hard work, demanding expertise in not only using correct methods but also exerting much labor to bring about desired effects of producing grain or animal life for the consumption of the world.

The Midwest is often called the "breadbasket of America." For the period from the nineteenth century to the twenty-first century, many changes in farming have taken place in both methods and equipment.

As the American settler moved westward and plowed the soil to make a life for his family, the early farmer often used wooden plows. When John Deere invented the steel plow in 1837, plowing became easier.

The early farmer depended on the horse or mule to plow, to harvest and to perform most farm-related activities. A walking plow and a one-horse plow were often the means used. These were used to cultivate the ground, bring in the harvest, store grain or hay in a mow and utilize the results to keep the farm in operation.

Wheat was, in early days, cut by hand, placed in shocks to shed the rain and later brought into the barns for the winter. In 1831, Cyrus H. McCormick developed the first commercially successful reaper, a horse-drawn machine that harvested wheat. Clover was cut by a horse-drawn mowing machine or sickle and made into windrows, later to be pitchforked onto a wagon to be taken to a barn, perhaps a bank barn. Then with horsepower and a singletree or doubletree, hay was elevated to the hayloft. From that hayloft, hay was thrown down for animal feed.

In 1839, the first threshing machine came to PawPaw Township in Wabash County, with Orlando Sowers as the owner. The Fordson tractor was another early machine; it had lug wheels. In Wabash in 1919, the

Before electricity, farm life could be daunting. Here a typical farm family of Wabash County shows off their livestock.

Wabash Tractor Company was formed and built a tractor similar to one of the Plano Tractor Company in Illinois. Called the Motox, it was powered by a Buda motor, weighed five thousand pounds and had a 1920 list price of $2,000; however, it does not appear after 1921 in Wabash. The *Plain Dealer* reported that local industrialist T.F. Vaughn broke ground for the new tractor factory in Wabash. Dedicated in October 1919, it was built on Manchester Avenue. Later, it became generally a sales agency for tractors. The company also sold plows, harrows, grain separators, hullers, ensilage cutters and road machinery. The advent of tractors revolutionized the agricultural industry.

The early farmer was an all-around worker who took pride in his surroundings and was often also found mowing along roadsides. Of course, fence tending also took a great portion of his time.

After the invention of the threshing machine, generally one farmer in an area was the man who owned a threshing ring and contracted with other farmers to thresh their grain. This also involved a threshing dinner, where all involved met for a meal to settle the costs of threshing. The owner of the rig went from farm to farm to harvest the grain. His rig consisted of a steam-powered engine and could be moved from farm to farm. Some early farmers also grew cowpeas—a forerunner of the

An early threshing ring in Wabash County. The women would cook for all those who worked with the ring.

Farmhands near Laketon in northwestern Wabash County. They are picking up freshly cut hay to store for their farm animals.

soybean—and a pea huller was used for this. That, too, was a forerunner of a combine.

Not just being a grain farmer, he also raised various kinds of livestock, not only for family use but for sale, too. Many farmers developed herds of breeding stock. Cattle were pastured during the summer and sometimes grain fed in winter. The family's collie dog was often trained to bring in cows for the night and for water. Providing water for livestock was another feature of farm life. Some farms were lucky to have springs or natural water sources. Others may have had to drill or use driven wells for watering. Water sometimes had to be pumped by hand. This writer can remember pumping water into a tank for cattle and then throwing down hay from a hay mow in a nearby barn and at the same time looking for that hobo who might be sleeping in the hay mow if a barn was near a railroad.

Another invention that saved the corn farmer many hours of labor was the invention of the corn picker, invented in 1850 by Edmund Quincy. Although simple in design at first, it became the magnificent invention of present day, with which a field of corn can be harvested in a very short time. Filled silos, either upright or ground silos, formed a farm source for utilizing corn for feed in the form of ensilage, then and now.

The early farmer saved seed from year to year, as these were the days before hybrids and use of chemicals for producing insect-free produce. The first grain elevator, built in 1842 by Joseph Dart, became a part of the farmer's life and still serves the farm today.

Machinery has made the difference in farming methods. Farming in the early days might be compared to the Amish farm operation of today, where use of horses is generally still the method used. However, even for the Amish, the use of battery-powered operations to control fences and pump water have changed.

The present farm operation is one controlled by mechanization, from the tractors to trucks; planting and harvesting still require the ability of the farmer as a manager. The Hoosier farmer's life is simpler and easier than that of the early 1800s, and use of diesel fuel is a part of present-day farming.

The one universal factor for farming yesterday and today is that of weather. It still is a factor that man cannot control but one to which he must adjust to the best of his ability.

———◦———

Roller Skating Becomes All the Rage

Today skating is all the rage. Many a young person in Wabash County has found roller skating liberating. The roots of skating in the county go back to 1879, when an advance agent appeared in Wabash to open a roller skating rink and encourage the citizens to become interested in the sport. Some local citizens thought that the agent was salaried by the American Medical Association in order to drum up business for local doctors.

The sport of roller skating started in London, England, in the year 1760. The sport spread slowly, but in 1863 an American, James Plimpton, had improved the skates, and it began to take off in the United States. The early skates used in Wabash were described by an early skater as "of exceedingly simple construction consisting merely of split shoemakers lasts, mounted on four boxwood casters, midway between which is a dufligger tomatus looking like an innocent can of tomato soap, but full of malice like a potato bug."

The first skating rink, originally called a parlor, was at the Harter's Opera House off Market Street. The entire floor of the opera house was made of wood and was satisfactory for skating. The seats were taken up, and the building was thrown open to the paying public on Mondays. Ladies had a session for themselves in the morning, and in the evening both sexes could enjoy skating. The manager of the rink was B.A. Tyre. He provided at a cost a large number of all sizes of roller skates. The public could come in and watch for free only during the evening.

Roller skating quickly became the most popular form of amusement among the better classes of Wabash society. People of all ages turned out to either skate or enjoy the ensuing show provided by those trying to learn. Many a belly laugh and uproar occurred when some distinguished citizen, like Doc DePuy, Hugh Hanna or Howe McGuire, cut a figure on the floor. It was claimed that the acrobatics on the skating floor from Wabash men outdid any circus in the United States.

Mr. Tyre provided instruction for those who needed it. He brought Miss Minnie Fenton from Indianapolis to give an exhibition of her proficiency on roller skates. She was only twelve at the time and demonstrated difficult feats, such as skating backward and circle skating. James Fenton, the roller skating champion at the time, gave a demonstration as well. Within two weeks, many Wabash skaters had become proficient on the skates, especially the young ladies, who always drew large crowds. It would take longer for the men. John Tyre was an expert of the fancy fall and made it into an art form. He would throw his body backward suddenly at a forty-five-degree angle. His left hand would fly behind him, as if to cushion his fall. At the same time, he would elevate his right arm. He would finish by kicking out his right leg horizontally while turning halfway around and waving his hands to the admiring crowd.

The roller skating parlor held a competition for the best male and female skaters; the winners would receive a silver cup. An award was also given to the worst skater. The whole town agreed that such an award would go to either A.L. Rohbock, Ave Davis, Jim Linn, Harve Woods, John Tyre, Howe McGuire, Hugh Hanna or Paul Herring. In fact, a special night was set for them to skate solo, doing difficult feats, including "cutting the pigeon wing."

A local tailor, George Johnson, said that there was a way to make money out of this new fad to hit the county. The agent who brought the idea of roller skating to Wabash told his victims—I mean clients—that if they stuffed their pants with large bathing sponges (at least eight) they could skate in comparative comfort. Taylor, however, put his talents to work and came up with a sort of rubber pillow attachment that could be sewn into one's pants. One day, he hired "Fatty Matthews" to try out his new invention. Fatty fell and the rubber pillow exploded. That was the end of the fortune Taylor thought he might make.

AN EARLY HALLOWEEN

On October 31, the Celts celebrated the eve of "The Day of the Dead." Over the years, with the spread of Christianity, October 31 became Halloween, or All Hallows' Eve, the day before All Saints' Day. Traditionally, on All Hallows' Eve, glowing lanterns, carved from turnips or gourds, were set on porches and in windows to welcome deceased loved ones and ward off evil spirits.

One Irish folk tale tells of a miserly man named Jack who played a trick on the devil. As his punishment, he was doomed to travel the earth until Judgment Day, carrying a chewed-out turnip glowing with a lump of coal, which the devil had thrown to him to light his way.

When Irish and Scottish immigrants settled in America, they brought their Halloween customs with them. In New England, they found pumpkins more plentiful than turnips and began to carve them.

The custom of Halloween came early to Wabash County and stayed. Today, the young dress up and collect candy. Sometimes, there have been costume parties with prizes given to the best dressed. Always there have been pranks. Outhouses have been turned over, sometimes with occupants inside. Bags of animal excrement have been left on porches and set afire. One ingenious person buried a store mannequin in a neighbor's garden. After a rain, it looked like a dead body coming out of the ground. One Halloween, a young man stretched a rope across the street about twelve feet from the ground. He made a scarecrow and attached it to the rope with pulleys. He stood out of sight and pulled the dummy across the street. He did this as a car approached to scare the driver. It worked for a while. One year, the students of the Wabash Junior High School History Club sold Halloween insurance to help protect property from vandals. If an insured house was vandalized, they would clean it up. But nothing today compares to an early Halloween in the 1880s, Wabash-style.

In 1882, the people of Wabash began celebrating at a very early hour—in fact the sun had not set. The racket that was made kept up into the small hours of the night. The town marshal had managed to get the revelers out of the downtown area, but no guards were set in the residential areas. Not only boys and young men but also girls engaged in all sorts of mischief, which in many cases amounted to actual damage to property. Street crossing signs were overturned, gates were stolen and broken, tree boxes were twisted out of shape and large stones were piled in the streets, while cabbages, potatoes and old brooms were thrown against doors. Fences all over the town were torn down, shutters on houses were slammed at all hours of the night and the Central School bell on Miami Street was rung with "great enthusiasm!"

The residence of Reverend William J. Vigus was attacked by a gang of youth who broke the screen door on the front porch and "indulged in horrible oaths and blasphemy" to annoy him. Harvey LaSalle opened his front door and blazed away with a revolver as the revelers approached his residence. Fortunately, he shot into the air.

At the Christian Church, the wood pile was tipped over, and the wood was carried into the street to create a fence running across Miami Street. Plate-glass windows all over town became targets as youths armed with stones heaved them through the windows.

All over town that Halloween, wagons left sitting out had the nut taken from one of their wheels, causing them to fall down when moved the next morning. Ah, those were the "good old days" so often spoken of.

A WILD RIDE

In 1869, Ed Beroth, Ed Tyner and Will Caldwell introduced the fair city of Wabash to the velocipede with dramatic results.

The enterprising entrepreneurs put the contraption on display, charging ten cents to look at it and, for the more daring, twenty-five cents for a half-hour ride. The velocipede, of course, was the forerunner of today's bicycle. Two wheels were connected tandem by a rod on which there was a saddle for the rider. Handlebars were connected to the front wheel. For power, the rider pushed himself along with his toes.

Beroth, Tyner and Caldwell saw the crowd milling about the contraption and saw their fortunes made. One brave Wabash man stepped forward and laid down twenty-five cents, wanting to ride this new-fangled vehicle. Out came the velocipede. At the proud direction of Ed Beroth, the young man listened carefully on how to control the new wonder. The crowd stood quiet, intent on every word. The young man pushed off, starting down Miami Street. When he crossed Market Street, two things became evident—first, a horse and buggy were approaching and second, Ed had forgotten to tell him how to stop. Flying like the wind through the intersection, the horse shied and became uncontrollable. The buggy overturned, dumping out its inhabitant. The velocipede hit the brick wall of the Payne Building, now known as the New Bradley Building, destroying the velocipede completely.

That was the one and only trip of the three men's velocipede, and it cost them $216: $100 for the machine, $40 for the plate-glass window broken by the horse, $5 for doctor bills, $11 for ruined pants of the rider and $60 for the runaway horse and damage to the buggy. Oh what great hopes for a fortune were lost in only seconds.

When you walk by the present Modoc store, if you look closely about ten brick rows up and five feet from the west end you can see a nick in the bricks where the velocipede hit.

Wabash's love affair with the bicycle continued. In 1883, high wheels made their way to Wabash. Those in Wabash tended to be sixty-inch wheels and cost about sixty dollars. The city fathers reacted to this new wonder of transportation. Perhaps remembering the velocipede incident, numerous ordinances were passed. One city ordinance forbade women from riding on the streets in "male attire," though a dress was fine. Women of Wabash were encouraged to ride tricycles, and Zoe Haas, the daughter of Abe Haas, had one of the first. Both high wheels and tricycles did not have a mass appeal.

Safety bikes, however, did. They were in Wabash by 1893. Theatre managers thought that the bikes would ruin their businesses. Young men organized races, particularly from Wabash to Lagro—the record being seventeen minutes and thirty-two seconds. They even organized the Wabash Dragon Club and took tours on Sundays to other communities. Young ladies, not to be outdone, began to ride bicycles. Doctors of Wabash became so alarmed that they might hurt themselves that they offered lessons on how to ride while wearing bloomers.

As always, the city fathers looked to safety in 1896 and passed an ordinance that bikes must carry a lantern at night. Churches also opposed them—particularly the Dunkard Church.

Bicycles continued to gain in importance, and it seemed that every young man in town had to have one. By the spring of 1930, just short of his ninth birthday, Rex Anderson had to have a bicycle. In his own words, he says that the "sections of our Sears and Montgomery Ward catalogues that advertised bikes, were dog eared and well worn. My parent's couldn't help but notice this, so they came up with a plan. I would go in the business of selling pop." The business would be financed with four dollars in his bank account. His father worked in a foundry "where it was very hot in the summer, especially when they fired the furnace and poured the molten metal." This would be the site of Rex's business.

"Our first move was to go to the local bottling company where we purchased a variety of flavors." His father took a washtub to work and stored it there. He also picked up a block of ice on the way to work. At midmorning, Rex would show up and sell the pop. By the end of summer, he had saved over twenty-nine dollars. His dad made up the difference. Since Wabash did not have a Wards or Sears store at that time, they went to Marion and bought a Hawthorne bicycle. It was royal blue with white trim and had all the features one would expect. The bike did not have a chain guard, so Rex would roll up his right pant leg and hold it up with a metal clip or just wear knickers.

⊷⊶

WABASH COUNTY'S LOVE AFFAIR

When did the citizens of Wabash County fall in love with the automobile? The exact date and first person to own one are unknown, but it was early. A look at some of the county records reveals some interesting facts.

We know that Arthur N. McCracken had the first Ford, but there were many other models being made. In August 1900, Hi Henry was hauled into the city marshal's office for "driving too fast on the streets of Wabash with a car." How fast the records don't reveal, but that was the very first speeding ticket.

In 1901, J.A. Bruner made front-page news when he received his brand-new Milwaukee Locomobile. It ran on steam power and was the first of its kind in Wabash County. Its tank held twelve gallons and could run sixty-five miles on one tank. The car and upholstery were dark green in color. Its "low wheels have spokes of heavy steel wire." At about the same time, Mr. Peabody of North Manchester had a car.

By 1902, J.L. Davis of LaFontaine bought a steamer from a dealer in Indianapolis. He began to drive the car back home at 4:00 p.m., expecting to reach LaFontaine by 8:30 p.m. Just outside of Indianapolis a rear tire burst; then about halfway home the other rear tire exploded. He tied the first tire to the rim, but after the second went bad, they were removed and the front tires moved to the back, which lightened the load a bit. He reached Marion shortly after 2:00 a.m., got a bite to eat and then started on. Eyewitnesses said that the car "left a long trail of steam behind it" as it left Marion.

Wabash countians love their cars. They have always taken good care of them. This is a scene in an early repair shop located on Canal Street.

Busy Main Street scene in North Manchester in the 1980s showing the number of cars parked in front of the businesses.

The first physician in the county to use a car in his practice was Dr. B.A. Houser of Somerset. It was a Haynes-Apperson, costing $1,300. This car was geared to run at the "unbelievable speed of 35 miles per hour." It was advertised as able to go "three times faster than a horse."

In 1907, there were twenty automobiles in the county, one of which was a Buick. In that same year, Captain Henley, a rural mail carrier, began using the automobile to deliver mail. Some say that this was the first such use in the state. By 1910, the entire rural forces were motorized. Frank Rettig learned to drive by going with Henley on his route. He would jump out of the car and put the mail in the boxes. One day, Henley backed the car into a rail fence and overturned the car. Both got out, turned it over and went on their way.

The Rettig name became synonymous with automobiles. In 1907, Lutz and Frank Jr. constructed a one-cylinder auto in their machine shop on the south side of town. The body was a buggy with a motor installed behind the seat. They used buggy wheels and bicycle sprockets. It was belt-driven and the gears were cut out of wood. When asked what they called it, Frank said, "Many names all of which are unprintable."

George O. Rettig liked to race. In the 1920s, the horse racing track at the North Manchester fairgrounds was turned into a racing track, not only for horses but for motorcycles and autos as well. On July 4, races would be held. Rettig entered the ten- and fifteen-mile auto races. He raced in an outdated Ford, fire engine red. His mechanics were Lamoine Ramer and Guy Forbes.

Automobiles had not been racing there very long. The track was a half-mile dirt track surrounded by just a farm fence, "and if you hit it, you went right through." The competition stirred up clouds of dust, but you "just put down your foot on the pedal and plowed ahead." Rettig won the ten-mile race with an average speed of forty miles per hour. It took fifteen minutes to go ten miles.

He edged out veteran driver Fred Galtry by only two feet. One person in the crowd said that "everyone was hooting and hollering for George because they knew he was just a young kid (17) driving against an older driver."

So who had the first car and when? We still don't know, but we're a little closer to finding out why Wabash loves its cars.

<hr>

A NIGHT AT THE MOVIES

By 1905, hundreds of stores had been turned into small movie theatres all throughout the country. Wabash was no exception. These popular nickela-show theatres, known as nickelodeons, were equipped with a projector, screen, wooden seats and a piano or violin. They became so popular that by 1908 there were nearly ten thousand of them. Wabash had its share.

Participating in this new form of entertainment were the Dickson brothers, Percy H. and William M. They saw the industry go from twelve-minute one-reelers to talkies and Technicolor.

The first theatre in Wabash was the Harter's Opera House. It was located on the upper floor of 75 West Market Street, later the home of J.C. Penney. This theatre was built between 1879 and 1880 and, until the completion of the Eagles Theatre, played all the roadshows that came to Wabash. It was originally equipped with gas footlights. It quickly adapted to the new flickering flicks, as the early movies were called. The Dickson brothers would add this to their chain in 1927.

At about the same time the Harter's was showing films, another nickelodeon was opened on East Market Street in the old Big Four building. Its name and who ran it is now shrouded in history, but it soon lost out to another located on Wabash Street just south of Market Street. It was located in a storefront owned by a Mr. Deardorff, who hired Floyd Schmalzried to manage it.

In 1908, the Dickson brothers came to Wabash and opened up the Dreamland, located a few doors south of the Family Theatre. The floors of both theatres were level and held about one hundred wooden folding chairs. The admission price was five cents, and the show consisted of one-reel motion pictures and an illustrated song, which lasted about twenty minutes.

Motion picture equipment was all hand operated and consisted of one picture machine with a carbon arc lamp and a rheostat to regulate the alternating current that fed the lamp. The one-reels shown consisted of faked newsreels, vaudeville skits and jittery travelogues.

The Dickson brothers eventually purchased the Family Theatre and closed it after a short time. In the meantime, they leased a building from Ruben Lutz at 18 West Market Street and opened the Orpheum. The Orpheum seated approximately two hundred patrons and was the first to use conventional theatre seating on a slanting floor. It was later enlarged to accommodate one hundred additional seats. It was at this time that two-reel pictures were being made, shortly followed by five-reel pictures. This necessitated two projection machines to keep the movie going without interruption.

Such movies as *Perils of Pauline*, *The Squaw Man*, *Tillie's Punctured Romance*, *Birth of the Nation* and *Intolerance* were shown in this theatre. Wabash audiences enjoyed William H. Hart; Douglas Fairbanks Sr.; Mary Pickford; Pearl White; John Bunny; Blanche Sweet; J. Warren Kerrigan; Wallace Reid;

The Eagles Theatre, located at Market and Miami Streets, was first built as a vaudeville theatre and later was used as a movie theatre. Dances were held in the ballroom on the top floor.

Mabel Normand; Wallace Beery; Fatty Arbuckle; the Gishes, Dorothy and Lillian; and a local boy from Rochester, Elmo Lincoln, who portrayed the very first Tarzan.

The Eagles Theatre played an important role in the movie history of Wabash. And it, too, became a Dickson brothers theatre. Built in 1905 by the Eagles Lodge, it was equipped with a large stage and was intended primarily for roadshows. The lodge operated it for a short time, with about one show per week.

Due to financial difficulties, the lodge gave up the theatre to the Yarnelle Realty Company, which leased the theatre to H.S. Logan. Logan upgraded the theatre for motion pictures with an occasional roadshow.

Logan ran the theatre for about three years, until it was leased to the Dickson brothers, who eventually purchased the building. With this new acquisition, they closed Dreamland. The Dicksons continued to show motion pictures, with roadshows and vaudeville on Friday and Saturday nights. One of the vaudeville shows placed the following ad in a local newspaper: "Introducing in a 15 minute act, juggling, unicycling, magic, hand balancing, ragtime piano and violin playing, dancing, globe rolling, wirewalking, talking and cartooning. Something original in each line. This one just a one-man act."

Also during the 1920s, Wabash High School put on plays in the theatre. And Coach Thom displayed his wrestling techniques against all comers, including Kenneth "Bill" Gray and other high school grapplers. The Dickson brothers continued with local talent shows and some traveling vaudeville for years even after talkies came on the scene.

Logan, not to be outdone, leased a room on West Market Street for a theatre and called it the Logan Theatre. This, too, was acquired by the brothers, who changed the name to the Colonial Theatre.

The Dickson brothers operated as a partnership for twenty-seven years, after which William Dickson was forced to retire. Percy continued to operate the theatre until 1942, when ill health forced him to retire as well.

WABASH'S FIRST HOSPITAL

In 1903, there was a great need for a hospital. Prior to this, several small hospitals, called such, were located in homes. In June 1903, a Miss Roser opened a hospital. A few weeks later, two young nurses leased the old Orphans Home and started a hospital. After operating it for several months, they gave up and moved away.

In June 1903, the entire medical force of several county physicians met with county commissioners to seek the use of the old Orphans Home building as a hospital. Again showing the power and influence of women, Anna McCrea began agitating the idea of converting the Orphans building into a hospital. She sought help from clubs, and the Clio club was one of the first to become involved.

The building was remodeled, and the first board of directors consisted of Miss McCrea, Mrs. Cowgill, Mrs. O.W. Conner, Mrs. B. Walter and Thomas McNamee. Mrs. Conner and Miss McCrea canvassed house to house soliciting funds. Some gave one dollar per week. Women sewed rag rugs, made curtains and contributed furnishings. They also made a trip to Chicago to get surgical supplies, beds and other items. Lodges and organizations helped. Dr. Rufus Blount, Dr. John Stewart and Dr. Lorin Smith also helped. Miss Jelly became head nurse. A hospital fund was also started via receipts of a ball game between lawyers and doctors held on June 30. Approximately $175 was netted.

It became a private institution. During the 1910s, there were many crises. Nurses were not always on duty, as there were no guarantees of payment. Poor management existed, the hospital was filled with patients and many troubles resulted. The Big Four Railroad even offered aid to keep it going.

In 1913, Dr. James Wilson and Dr. Gilbert LaSalle said that they would lease the building for a county hospital if Rose Thomas would accept the position as superintendent of the hospital. It came with the understanding that all doctors in the city might bring their patients there. So, in 1913, Rose Thomas accepted the position as superintendent, and the hospital became the Park Hospital. Originally from Grant County, she had been a visiting nurse, floor supervisor, superintendent of nurses, principal of a training school for nurses, teacher of Red Cross classes and trustee of the Indiana State Hospital Association.

In her book *Fifty Years of Nursing*, she wrote:

> *In the foreground are large oak trees; in the rear are orchards and gardens. The large vegetable garden was rented in shares; we received half—thus securing an abundance of vegetables for use. When I arrived, the hospital owned one cow. I purchased another and we had plenty of milk. I also bought hogs, which consumed the hospital garbage. At one time, I sold $500 worth of these. The night nurses also checked on the chickens at night. Fresh eggs and chickens were a great help in making out our menus, and we also used and canned many pears, cherries, etc. and made apple butter, jellies and jams. We really ran the farm to support the hospital.*

Rose Thomas also organized an accredited training school for nurses. Later the American Nurses Association did away with some of the small training schools, and they had to affiliate with larger hospitals. So Thomas took her first class—composed of Grace Fisher, Ada Strayer and her sister, Fern Thomas—to Grace Hospital in Detroit, as Indianapolis could not accommodate them. They adjusted well in a large city but sometimes got homesick as well as just plain sick. Ada Strayer became quite ill and had to be brought home. Fern developed diphtheria but recovered.

One incident Rose Thomas wrote about involved helping Dr. James Wilson give his son an anesthetic for an abdominal operation and also helping Dr. LaSalle with operating on his son for appendicitis. Again, quoting from her memoirs:

> *During the war came the terrible flu epidemic. At one time about half of the hospital force had the flu, but we were able to carry on. I remember two families of 9 each, brought in at the same time. A great many of the sick were not able to pay for hospital care; the doctors didn't know what to do. I consented to take these at the rate of $1.00 per day if the Red Cross would pay for them. We were delighted when the Service Motor Company gave us a check for $250.*

Quoting again from her stories:

> *A Chinese provincial student in Wabash was admitted to the hospital. He was working in the office of the Wabash Railroad Company. He took the flue and became seriously ill. He asked me to wire his uncle who lived in New York City. The uncle came to his bedside. The patient died and the uncle asked me to wire the Chinese Minister of Education in Washington, D.C. Immediately his reply was that he could not come, as he too had the flu. He wired me $500 and I was told to bury him in a metal casket and to place him in a vault so that he might be moved to China at the close of the war. We were also asked to keep the bill within the $500. An appropriate funeral service was held with Dr. Charles Little in charge.*

Another of her stories:

> *Elmer Burns stayed with us in the Park Hospital the longest period of time of any other patients—four months. Radios were not common in those days and the victrola was used a great deal for his entertainment. I recall one of his favorite pieces was "In the Gloaming," which we heard over and over and over.*

Rose Thomas decided to leave Wabash. When an opportunity arose to go to Wyoming, Thomas took the job and recommended Ada Strayer as her successor. Ada continued in this capacity for several years.

The Park Hospital served the community well. Many nurses saw duty there. Park Hospital was also the birthplace of Gene Stratton Monroe, granddaughter of Gene Stratton Porter. When the author called on her daughter while she was in the hospital, she gave her car and chauffeur over to the hospital nurses for short pleasure trips. The author herself spent some time listening to the birds as she stood on the back porch of the hospital.

In 1921, the county commissioners decided to build a new hospital on East Street with a nurses' home adjacent. Thus after sixteen years in operation, Park Hospital was closed.

THE KU KLUX KLAN IN WABASH

The Ku Klux Klan has appeared and disappeared more than four times throughout its history. White supremacy has always been its goal, but its anger and hatred was used against minority groups other than just black Americans.

The Ku Klux Klan rose to prominence in Indiana after World War I. It was composed of white Protestants of various levels economically, and by the 1920s, the group was against Catholics, Jews, African Americans, immorality and drinking. Nationally, Indiana was said to have the most powerful KKK. The peak of its importance occurred in the 1924 election of Edward Jackson for governor. However, by 1926, the scandal that surrounded D.C. Stephenson destroyed its image in law and order.

In a *Plain Dealer* article in November 1922, it was reported that the KKK had made its first appearance in Wabash County. Thirteen Klansmen marched into the LaFontaine Christian Church and down the aisle to the pulpit, where they lined up along the railing. The leader of that Klan group spoke briefly and handed the pastor two letters, one containing money, a gift from the organization, and the other a manuscript that the leader asked the pastor to read to the congregation. The leader said, "Brothers, let us pray." After the short prayer, the thirteen men, clad in white robes, filed out of the church to amazed looks on the faces of the congregation, who were speechless.

The preacher, Reverend McCune, then read the manuscript, which gave the purposes and ideals of the KKK, relating that it was strictly a true American organization upholding the principles for which the founders of our government stood. It also commended Reverend McCune for his good work in the community and recommended that he should continue his Christian duty there. It was not known whether the Klansmen were from Wabash or Grant County; however, LaFontaine residents believed that the majority of the thirteen white robed Klansmen were Wabash residents.

A year later on November 22, 1923, at the LaFontaine fair, the largest crowd of Klansmen ever gathered in town to observe Klan days, estimated to be from three hundred to four hundred masked Klansmen. They had a band with them and a parade of children.

And on the day before, 517 Klansmen formed a half-mile-long parade in the Wabash business district, with over 2,000 people attending. Klansmen came from Logansport, Elwood and Hartford City—some came on interurbans. The program started on the courthouse lawn with the Klan band and songs from the Logansport quartet. An Indianapolis woman and an Ohio man spoke of the purposes of the organization and about the KKK women's auxiliary, called Kamella.

In Wabash, the pastor of the Friends Church, Ira Dawes, was the organizer of the Klan in the county in 1922. He was also president of the Rotary Club, a man of dynamic personality and was well liked in the community. Formerly, he had been a minister of the Richvalley Brethren Church. A few other ministers were associated with the Klan, too, as well as persons from the North Manchester area. About 26 percent of the population of Wabash County belonged to the Klan at its height.

After the spectacular rise in membership in the 1920s, the scandal around the 1925 Indiana grand dragon, D.C. Stephenson, changed the impact of the Klan. Stephenson was tried and convicted of kidnapping and murdering a young woman named Madge Oberholtzer. After this scandal, the Klan collapsed, and the careers of numerous politicians who had supported the Klan also tumbled.

The first appearance in American history of the Klan was in the South between 1865 and 1872, started by a group of six men from Pulaski, Tennessee, mainly as a game of role-playing or wearing eerie costumes while riding on horseback. The first leader was an ex-Confederate general, and the Klan was filled with members of the recently defeated Confederate army. When President Woodrow Wilson, a southern Democrat, saw a film in 1915 that told of the Klan, he remarked that "it was all too terribly true." There was a rebirth of the organization after World War I.

By the late 1960s and '70s, efforts to revive the KKK were attempted, but generally such efforts have not been successful.

SNOWBALLS BUT NO SNOW: BLOOMERS AND BASKETBALL

It was the early 1920s, and the Wabash High School girls' basketball team, known as the Snowballs, ran out on the floor in bloomer-type outfits ready to meet their challengers. Their team had racked up quite a record as a winning team in the state of Indiana by that time.

In one game with Mount Vernon, the Snowballs appeared in these "bloomers" against the team in wool trunks. Those so-called trunks were longer by far than the trunks worn by boys' basketball teams today.

In those days, girls' basketball teams originally had five members and played on half courts. The center only played both ends of the floor, while guards protected only their end, and the forward could not cross the centerline of the half court. Sometime later, for a short time, nine-member teams were used on a floor divided into thirds.

The first girls' state basketball champions were the girls from Hobart in 1906. However, beginning at the turn of the century, Wabash High School began having strong girls' teams and played outstanding teams such as Fairmount, Huntingburg and Griffith, proving their abilities by winning more games and racking up state scoring records. A world record was set in 1930 when the Wabash Snowballs beat Fairmount 122–1. Member Billie Smyers scored 69 points and Beanie Davidson 53 points for that game. Wabash girls were undefeated at home from 1929 to 1932. At the state free throw contest in Bloomington in 1928, Wabash player Charlotte Engle scored forty-seven out of fifty free throws to win the competition.

Needless to say, their coach, Marcia Snow, proved to be a winning coach of girls' basketball teams at Wabash, which rivaled that of boys' teams. The name for the team came from the coach.

Bloomers, basketball and the Snowballs in Wabash proved to be an interesting part of Wabash athletics.

CIVILIAN CONSERVATION CORPS

On March 31, 1933, President Roosevelt signed a bill creating the Emergency Conservation Work Agency, later renamed the Civilian Conservation Corps. By 1943, more than three million young men had served in the CCC. The Department of Labor was in charge of recruiting for this program. To be considered, you had to be an unemployed, unmarried male ten to twenty-three years of age or a war veteran. Those selected were to spend a minimum of six months in the program or a maximum of two years. They were paid thirty dollars per month, of which twenty-five dollars was automatically sent to their families. Nineteen sites were selected for camps in Indiana. One was the Salamonie River State Forest.

In April 1935, the peak year for the CCC program, plans were underway for the creation of the Salamonie River State Forest by the Indiana Department of Conservation. The State of Indiana purchased the Oliver Shipley farm for an average price of $23.67 per acre. The worn-out farm consisted of 213 acres. Before the year's end, 180 more acres were added. The original 393 acres was barren, rocky, eroded land. By 1940, the forest would be expanded to almost 800 acres.

Shortly after the purchase, it was announced that a CCC camp was to be established there. In May, CCC Company 1543, from Marshall, Indiana, commanded by Elwyn T. Winks, was assigned the task of constructing the new camp. John Biggerstaff, son of Dr. James Biggerstaff of Wabash County, an officer in the army, was placed in charge of this detachment. While the camp was still in process of construction, Company 589 was sent to the newly instituted facility. This company had just finished all assigned projects at McCormicks Creek State Park when it was ordered to Salamonie. The company strength was 220. Dr. Edgar Black of Wabash was the company doctor.

The local camp consisted of a mess hall, an infirmary, a recreational hall, five barracks, a pump house, ECW quarters, a garage and a bathhouse. Before the bathhouse was completed, the men marched down a creek to a falls about a quarter of a mile from camp to take showers.

The camp at Salamonie was run similar to a military institution. The U.S. Army was in charge of camp administration and discipline. Reveille was sounded by bugle at 6:00 a.m. and retreat played at night as the flag was lowered. Personnel and camp inspections were held regularly. Once a month men were allowed to go into Lagro or Wabash to spend their five dollars.

Many enjoyed outdoor movies in Lagro. They were given five dollars in silver coins, which greatly helped the local economy.

Once living accommodations were established, the young men began converting the worn-out land into a state forest. It was to be a demonstration of reforestation, erosion control and land reforestation. They planted thousands of trees, both evergreen and hardwoods, and built access roads. A service building and shop, with an office on one end, was built. A shelter house with two large stone fireplaces was also constructed.

In October 1935, plans were underway to construct a dam across a stream flowing through the park. Lieutenant Kenneth R. Borgen, USNR, was in charge of the camp at this time, and F.A. Derck was in charge of the construction. When completed, an eleven-acre man-made lake, known as Hominy Ridge Lake, was created. It was one of sixteen constructed statewide.

In July 1940, the United States instituted a draft of young men into the armed services. The facilities once used by the CCC were turned over to the Civilian Service Camp. This would house people who objected to the draft. It was maintained by the Church of the Brethren for conscientious objectors from Illinois, Indiana, Ohio, Michigan and Pennsylvania. By late October 1941, there were one hundred objectors in the camp. They engaged in making further improvements to the park, soil conservation work and working on adjoining farms. The director of the Civilian Service Camp was Paul Bowman Jr.

Throughout the war, a forestry foreman and small labor crew remained. The camp buildings not occupied were used to store milkweed pods. It was thought these could be used in making life vests for the navy.

After the war, the site was used by local Boy Scouts as a camp. However, by the late 1940s, the buildings had been torn down. The lumber from the barracks was used to construct homes in the town of Lagro. Some were moved to the airport in Wabash.

On September 13, 1984, a plaque was placed at the site of the camp and dedicated by surviving members of CCC Camp 589. Beside the plaque are remains of the buildings, miles of footpaths, the lake and the seedlings planted so long ago that are now over sixty feet tall.

Wabash Women Served in War Times

The war years meant involvement of women as well as men in the service of the United States. During World War I and World War II, Wabash women made contributions toward the war effort in various ways. And since that time, women have continued to actively serve in various wars.

In 1917, Wabash's first hospital, the Park Hospital, was located on West Hill Street on the present site of the Women's Clubhouse and became a training center for army nurses. A *Plain Dealer* article in that same year stated that a needlework group of women made bandages for hospitals. By November of that year, women's clubs were organized into a federation of clubs to help in various ways. And by December 1917, war mothers met for relief work.

By 1918, nurses were recruited to work for the war effort, and in June 1918, Wabash teachers were asked to do war work during their summer school vacations. On June 19, 1918, the following Wabash teachers left for New Jersey to do clerical work for the government: Rose Coates, Hattie Waite, Emma Jane Conner, Florence and Geraldine Barton and Phoebe Lumaree.

The Red Cross ladies met at Roann in 1918 to sew. They used seventeen bolts of gauze and four bolts of muslin. They made sweaters, socks and other items for servicemen. In industry, the *Plain Dealer* of July 1918 stated that women were now doing work at the Service Motor Truck plant. Women also replaced men at the Wabash Cabinet Company. Women working in the Canning Factory in Wabash produced much of the products needed for the government.

In homes from 1917 to 1919, families had meat-less, wheat-less and pork-less days. Housewives had to manage meals without various commodities. Sugar was scarce, and housewives were limited to two pounds per family as sugar was needed for government use. Most families had victory gardens, conserving all items needed for the family.

World War II meant similar activities for Wabash women. Shortage existed and rationing was necessary. Generally, county teachers were in charge of rationing everything. They dispensed ration books with coupons for food. Teachers and other women rationed everything from sugar to butter, meat, gasoline and tires.

By 1942, in Wabash, the army swore in the first woman, Alice McNarney. Many women just graduating from colleges served as noncombatants in WAAC (Women's Army Auxiliary Corps) and WAVES (Women Accepted for

Volunteer Emergency Service). One Wabash High School librarian served as librarian at a naval air base at Corpus Christi and Beeville, Texas, as a civil service official. After a day at school back in the classrooms, she worked in the evening as a long-distance telephone operator taking priority calls all over the world. Still other female teachers worked in the summers, on weekends and after school doing secretarial work in Wabash factories. Women in Indiana also worked making parachutes at places like the Crane Ammunition Depot in southern Indiana. The nickname "Rosie the Riveter" became popular as a name given to women working in industry during World War II.

Women purchased and sold war bonds. They helped with scrap drives. Victory gardens were popular, and often women were left to produce vegetables for their families.

When Pearl Harbor was bombed, Evelyn M. Faurote joined the Army Nurse Corps. She enrolled at Garfield Park Community Hospital in Chicago. From there she went to Brigantine Island to get a taste of military life. She was taught the use of gas masks the hard way. Standing in a circle, the nurses grabbed their masks and put them on after a tear gas grenade was set off in their midst. After training, she was sent to Atlantic City until the time came to head overseas.

Faurote was then sent to England. She and others boarded a ship at New York and found that their stateroom had twenty-seven nurses piled into bunks three high and that all shared one bathroom. There were eighteen thousand troops aboard. They slept in eight-hour shifts—the beds were never empty. They were fed twice a day. The nurses were under strict orders to wear life preservers around their necks at all times. It took eight days to cross the Atlantic.

They landed in Scotland and took trains to England, where they were stationed with the 160th General Hospital. Faurote was assigned to a ward for soldiers with broken bones (the soldiers were separated by the types of wounds they had). After the bones healed, they were sent back to the front. "My greatest compliment I have ever gotten was from the man in charge of the wards of the 160th. He asked me how I got along with the fellows and I said 'OK.' He said, 'Don't be modest. Those fellows worship the ground you walk on.'"

After World War II, Faurote stayed in the reserves. During the Korean War, she was stationed at Fort Riley, Kansas. After serving fifteen years, she was discharged as a captain.

At the close of World War II, returning servicemen and servicewomen were entitled to their former jobs. It was at that time that the GI Bill of

Rights was established to give these men and women the privilege to obtain college degrees. College campuses were thronged with these returning veterans. It was necessary to provide Quonset huts to ease the overcrowding.

Women have served in various positions throughout past wars. From World War I to World War II to the present day, women have made contributions to society.

WABASH COUNTY CHEER CLUB, INC.

In 1958, Mary Good and friends saw the need for an organization to help the homebound. They began to organize a group dedicated to bringing a bit of sunshine into the lives of others. The result was the formation of the Wabash County Cheer Club, Inc., a service organization located in Wabash that has continued to be a blessing to countless individuals in the fifty years of its existence.

Cheer, Inc., is a planned program of services to individuals who are not physically able to get out of their homes. The articles of incorporation for the organization were recorded in the courthouse on May 14, 1959. Its stated purposes are to provide handicrafts for persons incapacitated; provide a workshops and craft center for shut-ins; sponsor craft and hobby shows; provide a lending library; and sell handicrafts. The articles were signed by members of the board of directors, including Howard K. Sundheimer, W.K. Delaplane, Ralph Sherping, Joe Nixon, Art Graebner, Robert R. McCallen, Mary Good, J. Robert Mitten, Wilbur Ford, Ruth Flynn, Olive Merryman, Marian Smith, Lola Vice, Bernice Hetzler and Irene Cleveland.

Mary Good, the first executive director, served until 1974 and was personally headquartered at 165 South Wabash Street. By 1975, Marilyn Forbes served as executive director.

In 1979, the officers were Donna Walker, director; Kathryn Clark, assistant director; Richard Rider, president; Mary Bizjack, vice-president; and Verl Steller, treasurer. There were 15 board members and some 1,100 shut-ins who were served by Cheer, Inc., in Wabash County. The organization held officer meetings four times a year.

In the 1980s, the mission stayed the same, but the location was changed to 9 East Canal Street, where it remained until 1991. Hillary Meek and Doug Lehman served as president of the organization at this time. In 1988, Lucille Moefler served as director. By 1991, June Coppock was director and lodged in new quarters at 405 South Wabash Street. In 1993, another move was made to 98 West Canal Street when Joe Richter was president.

Cheer, Inc., began taking handiwork to the homebound and handicapped, giving idle hands or minds something useful to do. Cheer, Inc., volunteers made visits to the homebound, bringing birthday mementoes and gifts made by volunteers at Easter and Christmas. These were to lift the spirits of those who might be lonely or in need of special assistance.

Services of Cheer, Inc., expanded to include volunteers delivering supplies to the homebound who wished to use their skills for making crafts, which were then sold to the public in the Cheer store. Funds received from the sale of crafts were returned to the person who created them to help supplement their income.

In 2002, Pat Kisner became the director of Cheer, Inc. The quarters were then located at 49 West Canal Street. In addition to crafts, the store carried home medical supplies, which were leased at no cost to persons who had a need for them but had no insurance or finances to pay for them. In that year there was such a large demand for equipment for hip and knee replacements that Cheer, Inc., began to work closely with "physical therapists and doctors to ensure the patient gets the proper equipment they need if they can't afford it," reported Mrs. Kisner. Along with assisting with medical equipment, Cheer, Inc., continued to make visits to the homebound.

Kisner created many of the crafts that were given as birthday gifts and made nearly all of the birthday visits herself, bringing along with her the gift of a small cake. She made between forty and fifty visits each month.

Volunteers were assigned a particular town in the county in which to make visits and deliver craft supplies. Each Christmas, over 1,800 gifts were created and delivered by Cheer, Inc., volunteers. Volunteers in 2002 included Lois Dixon, Ruby Gaston, Bonnie Kelly, Jane Dyson, Mary Novak, Connie Cook, Marge Summers, Marilyn Thompson, June Coppock, Dottie Force, Reverend Brian Hornbeck, volunteers from Whites and volunteers from Pathfinders. Kim Polk served as treasurer of the organization.

Pat Kisner retired on May 1, 2006, and since that time Cheer, Inc., has been under the capable direction of Cheryl A. Pinkerton Petro. She oversaw the move to new quarters at 18 West Canal Street. Cheer, Inc., still

Cheryl Petro, director of Cheer, Inc., an organization that helps shut-ins and has served Wabash County for fifty years.

continues many of its programs but now works with other county agencies providing people with information regarding assistance with food, housing, transportation and medical needs.

The Cheer store carries a variety of handmade items, including baby articles, decorative pillows, afghans, quilts, doilies, embroidery pieces, dishcloths, towels, birdhouses, canvas work, woodcarvings, jewelry pieces, candles and hair holders.

The Cheer store accepts donations of craft supplies that are used to assist the crafters who create the goods sold there. Items much in need are lace, fabric, thread, needles, ribbon and craft magazines.

Funding for Cheer, Inc., comes partially from grants from the Community Foundation of Wabash County and the Lutheran Foundation. United Way of Wabash County has been helping to support Cheer, Inc., for well over twenty-five years. Ilah Wagner, executive director of the United Way of Wabash County, noted at one time that "this is the only organization which does service like this." Donations from other area organizations and individuals also help keep Cheer, Inc., a viable organization.

Part II

Events and Happenings

———

From Out of Nowhere

Many and strange are the tales to be heard in Wabash County. One of the strangest comes from the first settlers of the county—the Miami Indians.

In 1825, C.C. Trowbridge was sent by Governor Lewis Cass to northern Indiana. His task was to investigate the culture of the Meearmeear (Miami) Indians along the Wabash River Valley. Trowbridge sought out two informants whom he held to be highly reliable and effective speakers for the Miami. They were Chiefs LeGres and Richardville. From them, Trowbridge gathered much of their oral traditions.

Chief LeGres, for whom Lagro was named, was living in the area in a brick house built by the government. LeGres had many interesting observations and much family history to pass on. One of the most fascinating dealt with his grandfather.

As a young man, LeGres's grandfather went with a party that was raiding another tribe. His thoughts were filled with the glory and honor he would receive upon a successful victory. Unfortunately, the rival tribe was stronger than anticipated. They put up a fierce defense of their village and drove out the Miami, who were forced to beat a hasty retreat.

In the thick of the battle, LeGres's grandfather received many severe blows. His body was covered with wounds from arrows and knives. His head appeared to have been literally hacked to pieces. His friends, fearing him mortally wounded, attempted to carry him away as they retreated.

The enemy continued their pursuit. Realizing that he was slowing down the others, he asked them to leave him to die. His only request was to be left against a tree facing his village so that his last sight would be in that direction. They obeyed his wishes and fled.

Late in the evening as he lay dying, something unexplainable occurred. A stranger appeared from out of nowhere. The stranger's countenance was unlike anything he had ever seen and frightened the wounded young man. The stranger was wrapped in shining plates of brass and iron from head to foot. The brightness blinded the brave as the stranger approached him. He bent down, pulled something from his body and stuffed it into the wounds, saving the life of the brave. He then disappeared as quickly as he had appeared.

The next day, the wounds had not only stopped bleeding but were also perfectly healed and featured no scars left. LeGres's grandfather's life had been spared, and he returned to his village, where he was looked upon as the recipient of a great miracle for the rest of his life.

Local Indian Sites

Wabash County is full of sites associated with the American Indian history of the state, such as the weir at Laketon used to trap fish. The lost silver mine locations are still unknown. The rapids of the Mississinewa below Somerset are held sacred, as is the home of the Black Panther that is still known to roam the county.

Hanging Rock is a limestone rock formation overhanging the Wabash River near the mouth of the Salamonie. At the top is a flat space about twenty feet square and approximately one hundred feet high overall. It gives a good look over the river and the valley below. Hanging Rock is a popular place for climbers. Years ago, Indians used to climb the rock to look over the area. Today, it is also a challenge for those interested in climbing.

The story is told that a Miami Indian maiden thought that she was in love with two Indian braves, both of whom were in love with her. However, she told the two that they would have to fight a duel at the top of Hanging Rock

Moon Rock is located on the original Indian trail that runs from Lafayette to Fort Wayne. A puddingstone carried down by the glaciers, it was held sacred by the Americans Indians.

and that the winner could then marry her while the loser would plunge to his death below.

The maiden climbed the rock at the appointed time. Secretly she loved one of the braves more than the other but wouldn't acknowledge it. The fight resulted in one brave falling over the rock edge and plunging to his death. The Indian brave who won the fight came over to the maiden to claim her as his bride. The maiden then screamed that she did not love him but loved the one he had killed. So she ran to edge of the rock and, seeing his bloodied and battered body, jumped over the edge to be with her true love.

About seven miles west of Hanging Rock is the Moon Rock. It is a great puddingstone that was carried down by the last glacier from somewhere in Canada. It is composed of irregular and angular lumps of granite, gneiss, syenite and other such rocks. It is fifteen feet long, twelve feet wide and over five feet high. It can be found on County Road 24 within the city limits of Wabash, just to the west of what used to be Cashway Lumber Company.

Many stories are associated with the Moon Rock. Its existence was first recorded by Major John F. Hamtramck, who visited it on a U.S. Army expedition to the area in March 1790. He had been ordered to the area by President Washington to record a description of the upper Wabash area. One story has it that the hoof print of a cow was once plainly visible on the stone, having been put there when the stone was found. Local citizens, for years, have carved their initials into the stone. Many marks are no longer visible, as the weight over the years has caused it to sink.

Local tradition says that the Moon Rock was a ceremonial center for American Indians. Awed by its great size and multicolored state, they would leave offerings of tobacco and such as they passed by. The rock was located on the main trail from Ke-Tong-ah (Fort Wayne) to Quiautonan (Lafayette).

Major Hamtramck also mentioned the "Hospital" in his 1790 report. It is located nearly opposite the Moon Rock on the south side of the Wabash River. It is also located directly north of the Friends Cemetery and is known locally as Shanty Falls. For years, this was the site of youthful revelry and picnicking. The Hospital is a cave about ten feet above the river and twenty feet from the rim of the escarpment. It is about three feet high and in the interior about wide enough for four men to lie down side by side.

Local tradition has it that an Indian out hunting was attacked by members of a rival tribe and left for dead. He crawled near the cave but, due to the seriousness of his wounds, passed out. An Indian maiden found him and dragged him into the cave. She cared for him, cleaning his wounds and finding him food. When his condition had so improved that he could care for himself, she left. By this time, he had fallen in love with her. Each day, he left the cave to search for her but in vain. He died pining for his lost love there in the cave.

THE LITTLE CUSS FROM WABASH

Before the canal and railroad, the flatboat moved goods down the Wabash. The flatboat was an ugly mass of lumber put together in such a way as to be buoyant under very heavy loads. Strength, not speed, was the prime objective in its construction. Immense loads of corn, pork and anything else were carried, and the crew was invariably made up of stout, hardy men who had three skills—"flat boating knowledge, a large capacity for drinking whiskey and a willingness to fight at the 'drop of a hat.'"

Wabash never rose to prominence as port of entry for flatboats. Lafayette had that honor. The Georgetown ripples that began several miles below Logansport and stretched within a mile of Logansport prevented the passage of flatboats. But the pirogue, which was simply an immense canoe, took the flatboat's place.

The crew of the pirogue consisted of two men, armed with pike poles, one standing at the stern directing the course of the craft while the other would push the boat along with the handle of the pike pole against his shoulder. This was hard work, and the men were always glad when night came, as that was the signal to pull into shore and "tie up." Reaching shore, the pirogue was made fast, after which came supper. Generally, supper consisted of corn bread, pork and coffee. The spice bushes were gathered up for a bed. Out came the pipes and whiskey bottles. Until sleep overtook them they smoked, drank and told stories.

In 1832, a number of pirogues were owned by Wabash County men, the most notable being Lewis Rogers at Lagro. His boat had a carrying capacity of two tons. Between 1832 and 1835, he along with Daniel Sayre carried hundreds of tons of freight. The trip downriver was always quite pleasant and was made in less than a day and a half. But the trip back called for harder work, often taking more than ten days. The pirogue would be poled back upstream or "bushwacked"—using overhanging tree limbs to pull the boat upstream.

The cost of transportation by this method was four dollars per one hundred pounds. Whiskey was an important staple for the crew. No pirogue was considered loaded and ready to take off until it had at least one barrel of whiskey aboard. And hard as it may be to believe, a full barrel would arrive and, when out of sight of man, Rogers and Sayre would take a quart bottle, fill it with water and then insert it in the bunghole neck down and let it remain until the water had run out and been filled with whiskey. Dan Sayre claimed to have exchanged barrels of whiskey in this manner.

Ben Marriner conceived of the idea of building a flatboat in 1834. He named it the *Eliza Jane*. He wanted to take it to New Orleans loaded with staves. Sayre and Rogers tried but failed to talk him out of it. Ben, full of youth and grit, set out one spring day to prove that he could do it. Everything went fine until he reached the Georgetown ripples. There the boat wrecked, imposing a heavy loss on Marriner. Pirogues continued to rule the upper Wabash.

Pirogue men and flatboaters didn't get along well with one another. Flatboat men tended to lord it over the pirogue men. Their mighty hero was Mike Fink, King of the River. When the two groups came into contact, a fight was sure to ensue. Dan Sayre was proud of his pirogue and at nineteen would take no "sass" from anyone. In Lafayette one year, a racket began when a flatboat man said in Sayre's presence, "I'm part alligator, part snappin' turtle and I can lick any damned pirogue poler on the Wabash." Sayre resented this and blows quickly followed. Sayre was a skillful wrestler and quickly clinched his opponent. Coming to the edge of the riverbank, the two men rolled down to the edge of the river. The braggart was unconscious with several ugly scalp wounds. The crowd sent up a cheer for Sayre; one grizzled old man led the cheers and shouted out, "Three cheers for the little cuss from Wabash." People crowded around to pinch Sayre's muscles and marveled at his ability as a "knocker."

What the crowd did not know was that as Sayre was rolling down the hill he had picked up a stone and struck the man severe blows on the head.

ROWDY WABASH

In early Wabash County, there was a criminal element that made life unpleasant. In the early 1830s, the Witt gang terrorized northeastern Indiana from its headquarters on Pony Creek, west of present-day Servia. They were horse thieves, counterfeiters and murderers. Pony Creek was named for the location where they kept their kidnapped horses.

Witt himself has been described as being about thirty years of age and weighing over two hundred pounds but being very muscular and powerful. He was known far and wide for his dissolute habits and would occasionally get drunk and raise quite a commotion. He liked playing cards and any game of chance. Miami Indians complained that their valuable horses were stolen by him. He would salt a field, attracting the horses, and then catch them. He is supposed to have died in a barroom fight near Indianapolis years later.

Events and Happenings

The record of criminals shows that the sheriff was busy with other forms of crime as well. Many prisoners in the jail were there for buying and selling liquor without a license, others for participating in riots (likely nothing more than a drunken brawl—a night in jail and a twenty-five-cent or one-dollar fine and all was forgiven).

Occasionally, there was horse racing, cursing or profaning Sundays by working. Young horsemen of the county liked to play a game very popular in Wabash County called Gander Pulling. Jeptha Sutton once faced charges for this in 1844. The young blades like Sutton would nail a gander through the web of the feet to the top of a post, and then the bird was won by the one who could ride by at breakneck speed, grab him by the head and pull him loose. Sutton received a fine of $2.87 for his merriment.

In 1849, a notorious family from the Narrows frequently visited Wabash, staying late into the night and making the night miserable for the inhabitants with their noise and carousing. They would chase people down the street while on horseback and ride into stores shooting their guns. One of the first ordinances of Wabash when first incorporated was aimed at this family, making fighting, whooping or great noise punishable with fines of two dollars for the first offense and three dollars for each subsequent offense. Records show that members of this family were arrested at least once per year from 1850 to 1857.

The first jail in which many of these criminals stayed was a two-story log cabin. To reach the cell, you went up to the second floor. A hole in the floor allowed for a ladder to place you into the cell. Straw was put on the floor to keep it clean. A slop jar was hauled up once a day. Food was lowered to the person. On February 18, 1850, the only inhabitant was an insane man. In order to keep warm, he pulled a board from the loft and put it in the stove. The stove door would not close, so he put the burning board in between the logs of the jail wall, setting it on fire. The community turned out and got the man out. A large portion of the crowd used the light from the fire to engage in a snowball fight. In March of that same year, the county commissioners agreed to build a new jail for $3,000. John Elliott and Henry Olin agreed to build it for $2,600.

THE DAY LOCAL DOCTORS BECAME BODY SNATCHERS

In the annals of Wabash County history, one story stands out. Every student at one time or another has heard of John Hubbard and the horrendous French family murders. The details of the story need not be repeated here, but suffice it to say that John paid for his misdeeds by being hanged on the courthouse lawn on December 13, 1855, at precisely 3:00 p.m.

But what happened after the hanging is a whole new story. Hangings were rare occasions in those days, and many would show up for it. Those who did had various reasons for being there. In the crowd that day in Wabash was a handful of men who wanted the body. Local doctors from Wabash and Somerset who thought medical knowledge might be enhanced by a study of the body hatched a plan to take the body from the grave.

The doctors took the sheriff into their confidence, and he promised to mark the grave so they could find it. After hanging Hubbard, the sheriff took the body out to the County Home for burial in the small cemetery about one hundred yards east from where the County Home used to be.

While the burial was taking place, word spread through the crowd that doctors from Fort Wayne and Huntington were coming to steal the body. The Wabash doctors, upon hearing this, began to set their plans in motion. A spring wagon with a good set of horses was hired from a local livery. At a fast pace, the doctors set out on their mission.

As they were going out Manchester Pike, clouds filled the sky and it began to rain. The doctors stopped the rig at a schoolhouse and began to walk about one-fourth of a mile back to the cemetery. In the darkness and rain, the doctors lost their way several times. It took nearly an hour to find the grave.

When they found the grave, duly marked by the sheriff, they realized they had forgotten their tools. One stood guard while the others went to get what they needed from the County Home. When they returned, the doctors from Fort Wayne and Huntington had arrived and filled an adjoining wood. Upon hearing the Wabash crowd, they began to yell threats and fire their guns, but the Wabash doctors stood their ground and carried the day.

The body snatchers turned their attention to their work. The soil in the newly dug grave was removed rapidly, and the casket was quickly opened, revealing Hubbard's body. A rope was tied around the neck and the body pulled out of its still warm casket.

Events and Happenings

A rail from the worm fence that surrounded the cemetery was utilized to tie the body and haul it back to the wagon. The doctors from Huntington and Fort Wayne left them alone; however, before they got to the wagon, one doctor carrying the body lost his footing and fell into a ravine, the corpse tumbling in on top of him.

Flying like the wind, the team of body-snatching doctors headed for Wabash secretly, or so they thought. Their plan was to use a building behind one of the doctor's offices on Canal Street to dissect the body. One doctor was left behind to arrange details. He would wait at the canal and get the body to the other side.

When the doctors reached the canal where it intersects Wabash Street, they found the doctor waiting. To get the body across the canal, a rope was thrown across and tied to the body. Hubbard was unceremoniously heaved into the canal, and the doctor hauled him in on the other side.

The body was dragged into the room set apart for the dissection. A party of men who occupied apartments in the building, hearing all the noise, went to investigate. They raised such a ruckus that the doctors packed Hubbard, or what was left of him, into a sack and toted him across the street in open daylight to a room where they might, or so they thought, do their work in peace.

After the dissection was completed, the doctors who assisted the work on the body divided the bones among themselves. Later, the bones passed into the possession of Dr. J.L. Dicken, who had them mounted and put on display in his office.

I wish the story ended there, but Dr. Dicken had apartments above his office. Tenants complained that at night the skeleton moved about, creating such a disturbance that they could not sleep. Either Hubbard had to go or they would. Dr. Dicken relented and gave the bones to LaFontaine High School. A few years later, the high school burned down; however, the science teacher had taken the bones home and put them in a shoe box. Somewhere is a closet or attic in which one might find poor Hubbard's bones.

VIOLENT DEATHS IN WABASH COUNTY

Since the early beginnings of Wabash County, there has been an element of the population who could, upon occasion, become violent. The Witt gang, living on Pony Creek, terrorized the surrounding counties. Coroner's inquests were constantly being held over unknown bodies found dead along the byways of the county. The following is just a quick review of some of the violent acts of murder that happened in the nineteenth century within the county.

On April 6, 1852, Jerry Means was killed by Abraham and Henry Hardin near Somerset. A dispute over a canoe led to the death. Means was beaten with a club and then stabbed. Henry escaped jail by dressing in his wife's clothing. Both brothers claimed to have been "seduced by the Devil" into committing the murder.

On May 7, 1853, Wa-Pe-Mungo was killed by Co-To-Mungo, being beaten and kicked to death by his friend about 1:00 a.m. after a disagreement while both were drinking heavily. His attorney claimed that since he was an Indian he could not be tried in the Wabash County court.

A log cabin in the Narrows, found just south of Lagro on the America Road, a scenic route in the area used by settlers and farmers to take goods to Wabash and Erie Canal. Home of the Joy family, found here.

Events and Happenings

On March 23, 1855, Edward Boyles was found murdered in the canal west of Wabash. This led to the arrest of John Hubbard for the murder. While in jail, he asked his wife about the family under the floor. Her reply led to her arrest and search of their home. The bodies of seven members of the French family were found. Hubbard was found guilty and is the only man to be hanged in Wabash County.

In the fall of 1857, William Joy roasted his infant son over a fire near Lagro. Joy lived in the Narrows near Lagro. He was found guilty and sent to the state penitentiary due to the testimony of his daughter.

In February 1859, John Luster was killed by David Blackman in a dispute over a card game. He was bashed in the head with an axe.

On January 18, 1863, Asbury Clark was riding on a train without paying. A brakeman hit him with a coupling pin. He was found dead in the snow by his father. The brakeman skipped out on bond.

Another murder occurred in March 1864. Mark Abbott was shot by Daniel Weizel of Company B, Forty-seventh Indiana Regiment. Both men had been drinking, along with others. Arguing over a man wearing a military coat, Weizel fired a gun at the man and Abbott. Abbott threatened to whip him; Weizel fired again. Abbott threatened to whip him again. Abbott said, "You ought not to have shot me" as he died. Weizel was sentenced to sixteen years at the state penitentiary.

Still another murder occurred on March 22, 1866. Dora Russell was accidentally shot by James van Ripper. Dora was playing with a pistol in a store, picked it up, pointed it at James and then put it down. James then picked it up and, pointing at Dora, pulled the trigger.

On September 20, 1866, Jesse van Dyne was being arrested by Marshall Wilson when Jesse pushed and hit him. Wilson hit him on the head with a cane, killing Van Dyne.

On August 16, 1868, Samantha Beebe Tumlin, fifteen years old and wife of Henry Tumlin, slit her throat. Henry, twenty-eight, had married his cousin. He was abusive and she was afraid of him. She finally left him and went to work in the Goodwin home on Hill Street. Henry wished to talk with her but she refused. He went to Hartkorn and Wolf's butcher shop and borrowed a knife. When found, he was lying on top of her with his arms wrapped around her.

On September 5, 1871, Mrs. Mary M. Finley, depressed after the death of her husband and worried about her future, killed her three children by bashing out their brains and slitting their throats. She slit her own throat while awaiting trial.

In February 1877, Leander Schrull was killed by Will McCowan. Both boys were ice skating during lunch recess at the McCowan School. They began calling each other names, and a fight ensued that led to the death of Schrull. Charged with manslaughter, McCowan fled the county.

On June 22, 1878, Alonzo Winan, also known as "Libe Hoog," was shot and killed while breaking into the store of E.T. Green at Ijamsville.

On July 11, 1879, Barney Abbot was shot and killed by John Dixon. Dixon was a watchman at the Wabash Railway Bridge. Both were drunk and began to argue. Dixon ordered him to leave; Abbot refused. Dixon then shot him in the throat. He was sentenced to five years at the state penitentiary.

Another violent death occurred on February 6, 1880, when Ephraim Pegg was hit in the head with a stone thrown by Walter Ophart. Pegg, walking down the middle of the road, refused to get out of the way of Ophart's wagon. A fight ensued. Ophart picked up a large rock and hit him on the head, fracturing the skull. Pegg died the next day while doing farm work. Ophart fled the county.

On February 11, 1885, William McGuire was shot and killed by newspaper editor Lee Linn on Canal Street. McGuire had made many threats against Linn. Linn shot him as he approached the office on Canal Street. The Catholic cemetery refused burial, as McGuire had not received absolution. He was to be buried at a potter's field in Lagro Township, but officials there also refused to bury him. Finally, he was buried at the International Order of Odd Fellows Lagro cemetery.

On July 29, 1886, William Bell (alias Lee) was knocked off a train by the brakeman, Samuel C. DeWitt, at Richvalley. The body was horribly mutilated. No charges were filed, and Bell was buried at the County Farm. The grave was later opened to get a lock of hair for his mother.

SNAKES IN EARLY WABASH

According to the 1914 *History of Wabash County*, there were subtle and dangerous enemies for the early inhabitants. Besides the rattlesnake, viper, adder and blood snake, there were a great many large blue and green snakes in the prairies. If you were to retreat, they would chase you. Although some of these snakes were harmless, they put people on guard against those that were dangerous, and their poisonous fangs were to be avoided.

Weesner's account in the same history gives this report:

> There was a great number of rattlesnakes hereabouts in those days. One day in going to Lagro on the tow path, I killed six large ones. On July 4, 1837, we celebrated the opening of the canal. I was called on to make a speech Saturday, and as the celebration was on Monday, the time for preparation was short. I wrote out the speech and on Sunday took a walk in the woods to commit it; when I nearly stepped on a rattlesnake and was considerably frightened at first, but managed to kill the reptile. A den of them was subsequently discovered along the canal while blasting.

From the county historian comes the story that one of the most interesting spots to visit in Lagro Township is a place known as the "old snake den," a short distance beyond what used to be the town of Dora, just off the old road known as the New Holland Pike. Here, in a little cavern in a rocky ledge, thousands of snakes used to gather and crawl into its warm dark recesses to lie during the winter months. Now Wabash County has several caverns, and each has its own history. There is Enyeart's Cave near Lagro, just up Enyeart's Creek. Then there is a cave at Shanty Falls, also called the Hospital, rich in Indian lore.

The snake den is special, though. You see, in the spring, thousands of snakes—black, garter, rattlers—would swarm out of the cave to the great annoyance of the residents of the neighboring countryside. One young man killed seventy in one day before tiring out. Another young man claimed to have been chased home by a thirty-foot snake. When he took his friends back to see it, he fully expected to see a cow being devoured by it. However, it was gone.

The men of the neighborhood had enough of the reptiles and decided to put an end to the nuisance, so one winter, while the snakes were sleeping, they built a high, tight board fence entirely enclosing the entrance to the den. Remains of this fence would still be seen into the 1880s.

Soon the warm days of spring began to penetrate into the cave, waking the sleeping serpents from their winter's respite. They began to wriggle out to sun themselves before starting off for their summer haunts. They quickly found that their home had been turned into a prison. Soon, settlers in the area came with guns, clubs and other weapons of destruction they could find. The slaughter began. The snakes tried everything to escape. They lashed themselves against the fence, and occasionally a long, big, black snake would almost reach the top of a post holding the fence when a charge of buckshot would bring him down. They tried to squeeze through small openings in the wall, only to be met with violence.

For over a week, the carnage continued. The actual number killed is not known, but one old-timer claimed that over a thousand snakes were wiped out. As late as the 1930s, people claimed that there were still great piles of snake bones to be found in the cave. One man claimed to have found the ribs of snakes that were four and a half inches in diameter. Many of the snakes found were over nine feet long. The fence seemed to keep the snakes contained and left the area depleted of snakes.

THE MONSTER AT LAKETON

There are many strange tales to be found in Wabash County: ghostly lights floating on the prairie, the black panther of the Salamonie and Mississinewa and the ghosts of Puckerbrush, to name a few. During the 1880s and 1890s, there were many snake stories being told throughout the county. Each community had its own story on the biggest snake, but none could outdo the snake at Laketon. It first appeared in 1880 and was seen every five years after that.

Laketon was a resort community. People from all over would head to Laketon and its lakes to relax during the heat of the summer months. On a pleasant day in August 1880, fifty people were enjoying fishing and picnicking on the banks of Long Lake. At first, a dark object was spotted basking itself in the sun, apparently unconscious. The milling crowd began to shout to one another. The noise frightened the creature and it took flight.

The head of the monster was much larger than a Queensware crate. It had a hooked bill not less than ten feet long. Its eyes, oval and sea green in color, were as large as meat platters. It had three legs on each side shaped like the legs of a crocodile, with terrible long claws.

It stretched out wings like those of a bat, fully fifty feet wide according to the eyewitnesses. Its body was encircled with yellow and black bands a foot in width. Boys in the crowd amused themselves by firing revolvers and shotguns at it until it became enraged.

It gave one shrill whistle, spread its ponderous wings and with a few oscillating motions raised high above the treetops. It then circled around the lake as the people below stood looking in amazement. After circling a few times, it plunged into the lake with a terrible noise.

One witness, John Thompson, was fortunate in securing a few outlines by actual measurement: 190 feet in length from tip to tip; 5 feet, 2 inches between the eyes; and a 45-foot girth. Believe it or not!

It was thought at the time that the Laketon monster traveled from one lake to another through subterranean passages, which were thought to connect the lakes of northern Indiana. It was also thought to have had similarities to the monster found in Rochester at Lake Manitou and painted by the famous Indian painter George Winter.

It has been a century since the Laketon monster terrorized Long Lake. The next time you are swimming at Long Lake and something touches your toes, ask yourself: Is it a myth? Or is it just waiting for the right moment?

—————

A HAUNTED HOUSE AND MYSTERIOUS
SITES AT PUCKERBRUSH

There is in the suburbs of Puckerbrush, just one half mile south of the public square on the regular mail route, an old house in a very dilapidated condition; there are no outbuildings except an old, solitary milk house, in front of which is a well with a bygone look about it; the well is tumbling in. The old-fashioned pump, which was made by one L. Wilsey when timber was no object, has long since become altogether useless—it lost its handle and all of its internal arrangements for raising the precious and life-sustaining fluid from the bottom of the well. Taken together, it is a very lonesome and uninviting place, bounded on the south and west by timber that has withstood the bleak winds of centuries.

On the north is the skeleton of an old sawmill that has succumbed to the ravages of time, a fit resort for the nocturnal visits of owls or bats; some distance to the east is an old house, looking a good deal the worse for wear, in which resides a family whose ancestors date back prior to the Revolution. With others, they were eyewitnesses to the facts that I am about to relate.

The house in question belongs to a wealthy family and has been used as a tenant house for a number of years, and it has been occupied by several different families, but these never had any mystery connected with them until the house was occupied by a family whom we will call Nimrod. But since that time, there have been frequent mysterious occurrences taking place witnessed by trustworthy persons.

Jefferson Brown states that in passing these premises after night—as his business frequently calls him to do—he has distinctly witnessed not fewer than five or six different times the appearance of a mysterious person standing near the house. His dress and attitude were always the same, except in one instance when a black hat, black pants and white shirt were his only attire; on every occasion he stood facing the public highway. The last time Brown observed this singular stranger, he was standing on the opposite side of the building and in size was that of a small boy.

On another occasion, the aforesaid Brown and Dr. Watson, on their return from Peru, witnessed one of the most wonderful phenomena on record just as they neared the premises, one that would try the nerves of the fearless. All of a sudden there appeared to rise, as it were, out of the earth, some kind of an animal, the appearance of which was that of a snow-white cow. Its horns were distinctly seen; it moved before them with noiseless tread for a considerable distance, and all at once it separated into thousands of pieces, every piece having snowy whiteness and diversified in shape. Dr. Watson is a disbeliever in spiritual visitants but confessed his inability to explain this away.

There are also other features connected with what has been related, more astounding, if possible, and bordering on the mysterious; they are beyond the powers of human comprehension. About one year ago, our informant, returning home from Marion late one very cold night and finding his family gone, concluded to go over to his neighbor Nimrod's residence and pass the night with his family. Waking up sometime in the latter part of the night from a very refreshing sleep, he was awaiting the appearance of morning when all at once there was a piercing and soul-rending cry right at his head, as if a female was in direst distress. And immediately there was a sound of a falling bullet at the front door rolling into the adjoining room.

On another occasion, while sitting in conversation with the occupants of the house in the full blaze of day, there was distinctly heard the trotting of a dog across the floor; at the same time there was a perceptible shaking of the floor.

And lastly, but not least, lights have frequently been seen passing to and fro about the premises—sometimes near the earth, sometimes up in the air—generally assuming the appearance of a man or a woman in full dress.

Here my story shall end. Oh, ye incredulous! Oh, ye skeptics! Ye who disbelieve in the supernatural. Oh, ye logicians with your great minds of lore! Will you turn a deaf ear and pronounce all things false that man in his finite capacity cannot fathom?

THE TOMBSTONE THAT MOVES

Just north of the town of Lagro is a cemetery at which many early settlers of the area are buried. Some of the many names are Abbott, Abernathy, Badger, Baker, Bartholomew, Bean, Bidwell, Burnsworth, Dare, Ditton, Enyeart, Harrell, Hillegas, Kelley and so on. Tombstones often take on different forms—one was that of Dr. John Renner, one of Lagro's early doctors.

Dr. Renner had come to Lagro in 1872 and became a member of the Indiana State Medical Society. Married twice, he had two children by his first wife, Mary de Rumple of Baltimore, and seven by his second wife, Jennie McVicker. Dr. Renner was a very popular doctor in the area, but he died in 1901 from Bright's disease and was laid to rest in the IOOF Cemetery at Lagro.

A monument to Dr. Renner was erected by Hugh Clark and is approximately five feet high about the base. A globe of high-polished

The gravestone of Dr. Renner, located at the Lagro Cemetery. It is said to be moving, but why?

granite about two feet in diameter and weighing almost nine hundred pounds was placed on top in a cuplike indentation three to four inches deep. It was quite a tribute to the well-liked doctor. On the bottom side, the globe was not polished.

Shortly after the gravestone was placed in the cemetery, the family began to notice that the globe was moving. The stone had revolved a distance one-third of its diameter. Hugh Clark, who had erected the tombstone, was contacted but could give no explanation to the mystery.

Various explanations were offered. One explanation came from a doctor friend of Renner's from Huntington, a Dr. McLin. He thought it dealt with a conversation the two had had on spiritualism. Dr. Renner had stated that if he died first, his spiritual powers would be recognized in some form. Others thought that the granite ball was magnetized by the iron casket in which Renner had been buried.

But was there really a mystery? A scientific explanation was eventually decided to be the answer. A close look at the cup in which the globe sits showed that it fills with water when it rains or snows; the sunshine heating one side melts the frost, and then the globe turns to the side for expansion.

Thus, year after year, the globe appears to be moving, which it is still doing today.

Intriguing as it seems, the movement of the globe on Dr. Renner's gravestone tells us that there is usually a reason and not just a mysterious occurrence. Just head up to the Lagro cemetery and decide if it is really a mystery or whether the scientific explanation is the likely cause. Or did Dr. Renner know something about the afterlife we don't know?

Part III

People

———◆◆———

The Hannah Thorpe Story

At one time, the tragic story of Hannah Thorpe was familiar to almost every family in southeast Indiana. The story reminded pioneer children to stay close to home and be very watchful.

Moses Thorpe was a farmer who had moved his family into the upper valley of the Whitewater River sometime before Indiana became a state in 1816. Their home was a lonely cabin about a mile from the nearest neighbors and surrounded by virgin forest and a couple acres of corn. One evening, the Thorpe children, having finished chores, were out playing near the cabin, when suddenly Hannah mysteriously disappeared. A diligent search turned up nothing. Upon close examination by expert hunters, fresh signs of Indians were discovered. These trails led to the White River country near present-day Muncie. No further trace was found of her.

Her parents never gave up hope of finding her. Mr. Thorpe spent years hunting for her among the Indian tribes of northern Indiana. Years would pass before he would find her.

Hannah grew up among her adopted people learning the skills necessary to the way of American Indian life. She learned to overcome the hardships she faced. Upon reaching a marriageable age, she married Captain Dixon. He was a Miami Indian and brother of Chief Meshingomesia. They lived near the mouth of Grant Creek where it enters the Mississinewa River, close to the region known as the Hog-back. It was here that the Thorpes found their daughter many years later. They visited with her for several days and tried to get her to return with them, which she would not do.

Captain Dixon had a reputation for being a shiftless, quarrelsome, drunken person. Most of his time was spent making Hannah's life unbearable, mistreating her. She had at least three children and doted on them. She even made sure they went to school. She was known throughout the neighborhood as a kind, affectionate person with family and neighbors. However, after one severe altercation with her husband, in a fit of despondency she climbed to the top of the Hog-back and plunged eighty feet or more to her death. She was buried in the side of the Hog-back close to where she died. Later, her body was moved to the community section of Mississinewa memorial cemetery. She is buried near her husband. A simple gravestone noting "Miss Dixon" marked her grave for years until Lamoine Marks had her grave marked with a plaque relating the details of her life.

Captain Dixon's demise wasn't so pleasant, either. Sometime in the 1850s, he was visiting Ashland, now LaFontaine, and had become drunk and involved in a fight. One of the participants in the fight picked up a hoe standing nearby and clobbered Dixon. Dixon received a severe gash on his forehead, exposing the skull. Dr. R.D. Mauzy dressed the wound and recommended that he be kept as still as possible. Dixon insisted that he be taken home. He was put on a sled and taken about two miles to his home. When he arrived, he was cold and stiff in death.

FRANCES SLOCUM

One of the most interesting Indian stories in the history of our area concerns the captivity of a five-year-old Quaker in Pennsylvania and the reunion with her family sixty years later.

On March 4, 1773, Frances Slocum was born to the Jonathan Slocum family living near Wilkes-Barre, Pennsylvania, on the Susquehanna River. The family were pacifist Quakers and had been friendly and fair with the American Indians around them.

People

After one Indian raid, Giles, son of Jonathan, accompanied an expedition sent to track down the Indians who had committed it. This he did without consent from his father. The Indians thought the family had betrayed them. On November 2, 1778, a band of marauding Indians attacked the Slocum household. Jonathan was working in the fields at the time. When they attacked, Frances, who had been playing with her three-year-old brother Joseph, hid under the stairway. Older sister May picked up Joseph and started running for the fort. Seeing how brave she was, the pursing Indians laughed and let her go. A neighbor, Nathan Kingsley, who had been grinding a knife in the yard, was shot and scalped.

As the Indians started to leave the house, one noticed Frances's feet at the bottom of the closet door under the stairway. He pulled her out, and another Indian carried off Wareham Kingsley, Nathan's younger brother.

The last view Mrs. Slocum had of Frances was that of her holding the hair out of her eyes with one hand and reaching for help with the other, crying, "Mother, Mother." Kingsley found his way back to his family after a few years with the Indians and reported that Frances was alive as far as he knew and being treated kindly. That was the last the family heard of Frances until 1835.

After her capture, she was adopted into the tribe and, with her foster parents, wandered for years through Pennsylvania, Ohio, Indiana, Michigan and Canada. She grew to adulthood and married a Delaware, who was mean to her, so she left him and rejoined her adoptive family.

One day, she found a badly wounded Indian and nursed him back to health. Afterward they were married. This was She-po-co-nah. After first living in Ke-Ki-on-ga (Fort Wayne), they moved to the Osage Village near the mouth of the Mississinewa. With his hearing and physical condition deteriorating, they finally settled at Deaf Man's Village on the Mississinewa. Here they lived with two daughters, Le-ke-nok-esh-wa and O-zah-shin-quah. The family possessed considerable land and livestock and had been able to save money from the government annuities they received. Their home was a double log cabin with two large rooms, a porch between and another smaller room at the end of the house.

In 1835, George W. Ewing, an Indian trader from Logansport, found himself near Deaf Man's Village. As night fell, he stopped at a homestead and asked if he could spend the night. He was given a gracious welcome, and the two Indian women of the family served him a fine dinner. The home was from all appearances a happy one and seemed to center on an old lady who stayed pretty much in the background. The members of the family treated her with great reverence and respect.

After the family had gone to bed, the old woman called to Ewing and indicated that she wanted to talk to him. As Ewing had worked with the Indians for many years, he spoke Miami, and the two were able to converse. To all appearances, the old woman seemed to be a typical Indian. She spoke Miami. Her hair was gray and her features wrinkled and wizened. She told Ewing that her name was "Ma-con-a-quah," which meant "Little Bear Woman" because she was so strong. Then she pulled up her shawl and showed Ewing a snow-white arm. Ewing was amazed and listened to her tale of captivity. She remembered her surname and thought her first name sounded like "Franca." She said that since she was old she wanted to tell her story to someone before she died. She did not wish to be separated from her family and cautioned Ewing not to tell anyone until after her death.

Ewing could not keep the story to himself and, as soon as he reached Logansport, wrote a letter to the postmaster of Lancaster, Pennsylvania. The postmistress thought the letter was so incredible she didn't believe it and laid it aside. Two years later, the post office was taken over by John Forney. The letter interested him and he had it published. The news finally reached the Slocum family, who wrote Ewing at once.

Plans were made to pay Frances a visit. Two brothers and a sister, Joseph, Isaac and Mary, traveled to Peru. There they met Frances. It began as a cool reception but soon she was identified. The discovery was complete when Joseph remembered that he had accidentally cut off the ends of Frances's fingers when she was playing around the blacksmith forge. Sure enough, she had the same stubs.

When the family returned east, they attempted to get Frances to go with them. She would not. Two years later, Joseph returned with two of his daughters, Hannah and Harriet. At this time, they were able to get George Winter to paint her portrait.

On March 9, 1847, at the age of seventy-four, Frances Slocum died. She was given a Christian burial but with much Indian influence and custom. A white flag was erected on top of her grave near those of her husband and two sons. In 1909, a monument, still standing, was erected to her memory.

INDIAN TRADER SAMUEL MCCLURE AND LIFE WITH THE INDIANS

Samuel McClure Jr. was one of a family of ten and lived with his father until about the age of twenty. Deciding to be an Indian trader, he went to live with W.G. and S.W. Ewing in 1828. In the fall of that year, he opened a trading post on the Wabash, two and a half miles from the mouth of the Mississinewa. At that time, he learned the Indian language and gained their confidence.

During the winter of 1832, he moved his trading post to three miles below Wabash, on his father's farm. In 1833, Samuel and his brother Robert cut the first state road running through Wabash County. The road ran from the twenty-mile stake in Wabash County to the town of Wabash and on to North Manchester. This was done at a cost of $7.58 per mile. On January 10, 1833, Samuel married Susannah Furrow of Fort Laramine, Ohio.

In February 1834, he moved to Marion, where he engaged in trading with the Meshingomesia band. There he remained, dealing with the Indians. In the words of interviewer Thad Butler, the following are the stories of the Indians and of Samuel McClure.

Fifty years ago, near the mouth of the Mississinewa River, about four miles east of Peru, stood the largest village of the Miami tribe of Indians. It was known as the Asash Village, and was the residence of Asash the war chief of the tribe. It was here that the grand councils of the tribe were held, attended by the great men of the entire tribe from Fort Wayne to Lafayette, and presided over by John Baptiste Richardville, the national chief, a well-educated half breed Frenchman. It was the "capital" of the Miami Nation, and in 1828, the Ewings of Fort Wayne, then the great Indian traders of the Wabash Valley, concluded to open a trading post near this point. They designated as the person to have charge of the post a young man in their employ by the name of Samuel McClure who was a well-respected citizen of Marion and probably the only living survivor of those who entered the wilderness in the early days for the purpose of opening traffic with the Indian.

Mr. McClure was a thorough master of the Miami language and recalled the names of Indians readily as other old settlers would those of white acquaintances. He knew the father of Chief Me-Shin-go-me-sia, To-cin-you, and said that his ancestors were the great men of the tribe beginning of this century. Me-shin-go-me-sia's grandfather, Pe-con-ge-oh,

visited Gen. Washington when he was president of the United States, and
Oz-an-di-ah, father of Pecon-ge-oh, was the great national chief of the
Miamis about the time of the Revolutionary War. Their great councils
were then held near Piqua, Ohio, and their country embraced a large scope
of territory. LaGros, after whom the village of LaGro was named, resided
at Greenville, Ohio and was a prominent Indian figure.

Mr. McClure was a witness of many gatherings of the Indians, and
attended every Indian payment made by the government since 1830. In council,
Me-shin-go-me-sia, after the death of his father, sat at the right hand of Chief
Pe-she-wah, and was rated highly, but the man whose good will was most
courted, and hatred feared, was Big Majenica. He was a terror to the whites
and tyrant among his own people. When his suggestions were not followed, he
would suddenly withdraw from the council. Al-lo-lah, whose village was just
south of Wabash, was described as a good, social and clever Indian, while
Osash, the war chief, was a mild mannered man, small of stature, who wore
a broad-brimmed hat, and had every appearance of a Quaker.

LaFontaine, father of Chief Lafontaine, was a half-breed Frenchman, a
good writer, and well-educated, as was also Joe Richardville, brother of the
chief, and who had the further accomplishment of fiddle and flute playing.
Pol-zo-wah, alias Frank Godfroy succeeded Osash as war chief, and his
descendants still remain in the area.

The Indians lived in peace with both the whites and neighboring
tribes after Mr. McClure knew them. The Wea or Eel River Band had
some trouble after they sold their lands and removed from Tippecanoe
County to the Eel River country, and were quite hostile. The Miamis and
Pottawatomies would sometimes assemble on opposite sides of the river and
celebrate some even in Indian history, and such gatherings often ended in
tragedy. The custom was then a life for a life, or a gift to the family. Pe-she-
wah was stabbed and killed by a Pottawatomie, and his family refused to
compromise until they received the handsome sum of $5,000.

The principal commodities purchased of the Indians by Mr. McClure
were the skins of bear, raccoon, otter and muskrat. These the trader gathered
by trips through the wilderness on horseback, and many were the hardships
endured. One March, Mr. McClure froze his feet very badly, having to
wade through the river, and narrowly escaped death two or three times.
Once, an Indian known as "the Hunter" came to the trading post with
Richardville. The "Hunter" helped himself pretty freely with liquor, and
got desperately drunk. It was while in this condition that he attempted
to shoot McClure, who, with the aid of Richardville, tied the would-be

murderer and held him prisoner until he became sober. The "Hunter" was very sorry for his conduct, and ever after kept sober. A drunken Indian once broke into the store and began helping himself to whiskey, when McClure knocked him down with a club. The assault offended the wife of the Indian, who for some time refused to trade with him, until he made her a present of two bunches of worsted yarn, after which she became a very ardent friend.

Mr. McClure attended Indian burials frequently. He was present at the funeral of Chap-en-do-ce-oh, a brother of Chief Me-shin-go-me-sia. The chief had been appointed to make a speech at the grave, but was so affected that he nearly broke down, when Wah-pe-s-tah, another brother, reproved him for "playing the woman." The chief then calmly proceeded with the oration. There was no particular marriage ceremony among the Miamis, but after a couple had signified their intention to live together, there was an exchange of presents, and the compact was ratified by the approval of the girl's parents. Generally, the Indians were true to each other, and death only broke up the family relation. The Miamis had about the same religious ideas as other North American Indians. One of their traditions seemed to confirm the account of the flood, except that instead of the dove notifying the survivors of the receding flood, "a crawfish came up and gave them the sign that the waters were going away."

When Mr. McClure first knew the Miamis, they numbered between two and three thousand. Samuel McClure had their unlimited confidence, and his stories of dealing with the tribe have given a picture of their lives and values unknown today.

—◦◦◦—

CAPTAIN GESS, MIGHTY INDIAN FIGHTER

On February 17, 1835, a two-wagon emigrant train from Connersville, Indiana, arrived at the Wabash River close to the site of the Wabash Street Bridge. The wagons consisted of several teams, the largest belonging to William Gess of Fayette County. The Wabash River was frozen over, and Gess decided to drive his wagon across the ice. Before he proceeded far, one of the wheels of his wagon went through the ice. They rightfully decided to camp for the night on the south side of the river. They unhitched their horses and cared for them through the night and then commenced looking about with a view to provide for their comforts. Dry timber was soon found, and a blazing, cheerful fire made them more comfortable.

A rude tent was constructed of blankets, and after cooking and eating some supper, the party was ready to seat themselves around the fire and indulge in campfire conversation or tale-telling. Before all this had been done, the women and children of the party had been taken to the residence of Daniel Jackson, where they were kindly cared for during the night.

Not far from where they camped, in fact on the hill directly above them, was the Miami Indian village of Black Loon.

That evening, the men sat around the campfire enjoying their pipes and tales. Being so near to Black Loon's village, the stories naturally turned to Indian wars and adventures related to them. Gess, who was an old Kentuckian, took special delight in them, as he was descended from a race of Indian fighters and claimed to have shot a few himself.

Gess worked up the party into a terrible state of alarm by depicting some of the bloody deeds in "Ole Kaintuck" and the massacre at Pigeon Roost. He had worked the boys around the fire into such a state that they concluded they must keep a guard on duty during the night. It was decided that they should be on duty one hour each.

One of the party, an eighteen-year-old youth, happened to be standing watch at midnight. A short time after he had taken his post, he heard the Indians coming down the hill toward the camp. Their footsteps breaking through the crust of the snow could be heard with alarming distinctness, and he rushed to the camp to arouse his slumbering comrades. He informed them that the Indians were coming, and immediately preparations were made to give the "redskins" a warm reception.

Gess quickly took command. He gave orders rapidly as to what should be done with the teams and left some bequests to his wife and little ones in case he should fall in the battle about to be fought. Then, arming himself with the only gun in the party and placing chopping axes in the hands of others, he commanded silence until the approach of the Indians or further orders from him. The guard who had spread the alarm took his stand at the back of a tent, expecting to come face to face with the fearsome foe any minute.

The enemy continued to advance their footsteps in the snow, getting closer and closer. They halted for a moment and then advanced again. One of the enemy slipped cautiously to the back portion of the tent and was in the process of lifting the blanket when the young man, summoning all his courage, raised the axe on high and dealt the intruder a blow on the head that made him bellow with pain and beat a hasty retreat. An examination of the axe revealed the presence of blood and hair, and there was no doubt in the tent as to the fact that an Indian had been killed.

Captain Gess prepared the men for a return, keeping them ever vigilant and on guard. None returned. The following morning, the men sallied forth for the purpose of tracking the Indian who had attempted their destruction. They followed a trail of blood to the top of the hill where, to their amazing surprise, instead of an Indian they found some half-starved cows, one of which was bleeding from the forehead.

Captain Gess returned to camp much more docile, as well as a wiser individual. He returned to spend his days in "Ole Kaintuck," where it was much tamer.

First Wabash Resident to Enlist in the Civil War

One of the first great statesmen in Wabash history was also one of the city's first great military leaders and in fact was probably the first city resident to sign up for the Civil War.

Charles Sherman Parrish, the son of Orris and Amelia Parrish, was born in Columbus, Ohio, on May 25, 1830. At the age of eight, his father (a lawyer and judge) died, and the family moved to Delaware, Ohio. It was there that Parrish attended a select school, and he later went on to Ohio Wesleyan University and Kenyon College.

In 1847, the seventeen-year-old entered the law office of Searle and Cox, and four years later he was admitted to the bar. After a stay in Greensburg, Indiana, he came to Wabash in 1854 and two years later was admitted to the city's bar. In 1856, his public career began when he was elected prosecuting attorney, a position he held until December 1, 1858. In November 1857, he also was co-owner of the *Wabash Intelligencer* and remained so until April

1858. In 1858, he entered into partnership with J.D. Conner and remained until the outbreak of the Civil War.

Parrish was militarily inclined even before the war. In 1857, he organized a local militia known as the Wabash Guards. With his background, it was only natural that on April 13, 1861, only one day after the firing upon Fort Sumter, he opened a recruiting office and enrolled 150 men. These men were mustered into the Eighth Indiana Regiment at Indianapolis on April 25, 1861, as Company H, with Parrish as captain of the regiment.

Parrish wasn't finished when the company was mustered out. He quickly reenlisted for three years as a major. In May 1863, he was commissioned as lieutenant colonel. He remained with the 8th until promoted to colonel with command of the 130th Indiana Regiment. The 130th was mustered in on March 12, 1864, and remained in service until December 2, 1865. On March 13, 1865, Parris was promoted to brevet brigadier general.

After the war, Parrish returned to Wabash and resumed his law practice. In 1867 and 1868, he was elected state senator for Wabash and Kosciusko Counties. In 1868, he accepted the appointment of register in bankruptcy, which he held until 1869, when he resigned to become inspector of customs at New Orleans. He held this position until 1873, when he returned to Wabash.

Five years later, Parrish was elected mayor of the city, holding the position until 1882. He was mayor at the time Wabash became the first electrically lighted city in the world. General Parrish claimed that he could read the newspaper on his front porch on the northeast corner of Hill and Comstock Streets, due to the brilliant light produced by the arc lights.

Parrish was also involved in his community socially. On September 1, 1866, Encampment Post Number 1 of the Grand Army of the Republic was formed in Wabash, with Parrish serving as its first commander. He was also a charter member of the James Emmett Post No. 6 of the GAR.

Parrish was married to Annie Cox, the daughter of Reverend Samuel Cox, on July 27, 1859. Three children were born to the couple: Annie M., Cornelia J. and Sherman, the last of whom died at the age of three. Parrish left Wabash in 1892 and lived in a soldier's home in Tennessee. In 1907, word was received that Parrish had died in a soldier's home in Galena, Kansas, near where he had family. Gone was a man whose courage and military spirit were phenomenal. He was the first soldier to enlist, the first captain, the first major, the first lieutenant colonel and the only full colonel to go from Wabash County to the field of battle during the Civil War.

ADELAIDE STEELE BAYLOR

Born in Wabash in the 1860s, Adelaide Steele Baylor was a graduate of Wabash High School in 1878. She then became a teacher, an elementary school principal, an assistant principal (later principal) of the Wabash High School and after that superintendent of Wabash City Schools. From that date, she joined in 1911 the staff of the Indiana state superintendent of education.

Adelaide Steele Baylor was named for her grandfather, Colonel William Steele, one of Wabash's founding fathers. Her father, Jim Baylor, was an attorney but was addicted to alcohol and so had many problems. A lady who knew the family stated that at times Adelaide would have to go downtown and "walk" her father home.

As a young person, Adelaide was a lover of books and an avid reader. Active in the Presbyterian Church as she grew up, she later became involved in temperance work.

Adelaide Steele Baylor, student, teacher, principal and superintendent for the Wabash City Schools. She worked at the State Department of Education and in Washington, D.C.

After graduating from Wabash High School, she began teaching in the city's elementary schools, where she was a teacher from 1878 to 1884. Then she became assistant principal at the high school and later became principal, a position she held until 1903. From 1903 to 1911 she served as superintendent of the Wabash City Schools.

In 1911, Adelaide joined the Indiana State Department of Education as assistant superintendent of instruction. Interested in vocational education, in 1918 she was named a member of the Home Economics Educators Service Staff, a position under the Federal Board of Vocational Education. In 1919, she supervised studies in twenty-five states. By 1923, she had become chief of that division, which involved her traveling to many states, as well as Hawaii and Puerto Rico.

Adelaide Steele Baylor was the only woman (as of 1942) ever suggested as state superintendent of public instruction in Indiana, a position she declined. However, at one time, she was president of the Indiana City and State Department Association of Superintendents. She was also instrumental in organizing the Parent Teachers Association.

Adelaide Steele Baylor did her undergraduate work at Michigan and the University of Chicago, where she was given an honorary degree. She received a scholarship from Columbia University in 1918.

On October 30, 1935, she retired as chief of the Home Economics Education Service, and a few weeks later she died. She is buried at Falls Cemetery, Wabash. A painting of her was hung in the Wabash High School Library in a building named for her.

———

MEDICAL HEROES: THE WAGNER BROTHERS

In the annals of medical science, two names have been lost to time. Two Hoosiers, both brothers, sacrificed themselves in the attempt to advance and perfect what we now take for granted—X-rays. Both died young due to overexposure to the harmful rays and are truly martyrs.

Thurman L. Wagner was the son of Joseph and Livina Wagner. He was born in the small community of Treaty just a few miles south of Wabash in 1876. His father owned and operated a sawmill. The family moved to Roann and then to the city of Wabash. Thurman's older brother was Rome V. Wagner, and their lives intertwined. In 1887 and 1888, Rome attended Central Normal College at Danville, followed by entrance to the Central College of Physicians and Surgeons in Indianapolis. After graduation in 1889, he moved to Chicago.

In 1895, Thurman graduated from Wabash High School and, following in his brother's footsteps, became an assistant in the office of a local physician. Rome helped his brother attend the College of Physicians and Surgeons in Chicago, graduating after attending night classes at Jenner Medical College. While studying to be a doctor, Thurman became interested in the work of his brother. Rome had founded the R.V. Wagner Company, which sold electrical apparatus for medical purposes, such as the mica-plate static machine he had invented. This machine became his major contribution to the operative equipment of radiology.

Rome invented, with Thurman's help, a number of X-ray appliances. Among the brothers' achievements were the very first X-ray photographs taken in the United States. Their company was known, at the time, as one of the largest of its kind in the country. Both brothers would travel around the United States demonstrating the feasibility and potential use of X-rays. They would often serve as human guinea pigs during these demonstrations.

In 1902, while giving a demonstration, Thurman was seriously burned by X-rays. He kept this to himself. In 1903, Rome was severely burned and sent a telegram to warn Thurman of the effects and to be careful. Both brothers developed severe lesions on those parts of their bodies that had been exposed. Rome was mostly affected on his face and hands and Thurman on his hands and back. Thurman would lose three fingers on his right hand, and eventually the entire hand would be removed.

Both Rome and Thurman suffered terribly but did not give up. They found solace in each other. They could often be found walking together or singing songs while walking the floor in pain. Rome's suffering ended on March 19, 1908, in Chicago. He is now buried in Falls Cemetery, Wabash.

Thurman would live on for four more years. He continued his brother's work and was the head of the R.V. Wagner Company. Due to the exposure he had received, he also soon passed away. He died in St. Louis on May 28, 1912, and was buried in Hoover Cemetery, Cass County, Indiana.

A MARTYR TO SCIENCE

At the beginning of the Spanish-American War, a young man desperately wanted to enlist and fight for his county. His name was John R. Kissinger. He was from the Liberty Mills area of Wabash County. He managed to enlist in Company D of the 157th Indiana Volunteers. However, fate had another plan for him.

While the company was stationed in Indianapolis, Captain B.F. Clemans was ordered to send two men to the hospital to aid in nursing the sick. Among those volunteering to go was Private John R. Kissinger. Kissinger proved to be a very capable nurse, and when the regiment returned from a furlough, he was kept in the hospital until discharged. The next day, he enlisted in the regular army as a private in the hospital corps.

He got his wish to get to Cuba but not to see action. He was sent to the Columbia barracks at Quemadoes, nine and a half miles from Havana, where he served as an acting hospital steward. Here he became involved with doctors seeking the cure for diseases that the military had to contend with in Cuba, among them yellow fever.

The medical authorities in charge of the hospital there were interested in the causes and treatments of this dreaded disease. Whether yellow fever was inoculated or carried in clothing was unknown. The doctors proposed to experiment on a number of animals. Kissinger, overhearing their discussions and realizing its importance to the medical profession, volunteered to go through the ordeal. After getting permission from high up the chain of command, Kissinger was accepted along with others for the experiment. He was told that he would be paid for what he did. With his characteristic modesty, he replied that he was not doing this for money but for the sake of science and the cause of humanity.

Dr. Walter Reed was in charge of the experimentation. He placed a number of female mosquitoes in a room with yellow fever victims, and as soon as the insects had filled themselves with the blood of the sufferers, they were placed in a jar for safekeeping. After twelve days' time, they were placed in a room with Kissinger and allowed to bite him. This was done several times with no results. The last time they were allowed to bite him, he came down with the fever.

After a severe bout of yellow fever, he recovered. A month later, blood was taken from a victim of the fever and injected into him. It affected him in no way and showed that he was immune to yellow fever. Besides Dr. Walter Reed, doctors from Germany, Spain and Cuba were interested in the experiment.

Upon Kissinger's complete recovery, the medical authorities presented him with a solid gold watch as a mark of their esteem for him. This watch was engraved "John R. Kissinger, For Courage." He was also promoted from a private in the hospital corps to the rank of acting hospital steward. After three months' furlough, during which he returned to Wabash County, he returned to Governors' Island, New York, where he was discharged seven months later.

He later returned home. His health began to fail, and he lost the use of his legs. He moved to South Bend, Indiana, where he and his wife took in laundry. He was a common sight on the streets, pushing himself around on a specially made cart with laundry in tow.

With the publicity surrounding the movie *Yellow Jack*, released in the 1930s, Kissinger's plight came to the attention of the government. He was awarded the Congressional Medal of Honor for volunteering for this experiment. He was only the second man in Wabash County to receive the honor. The American Medical Association also presented him with a house in Huntington County, where he spent the rest of his life.

LOREN M. BERRY

The story of the Yellow Pages begins in the Midwest about 1910. Today countless thousands make regular referrals to this reference source. The founder, Loren M. Berry, was born in Wabash on July 14, 1888. Both of his parents had been reared on Wabash County farms. When he was born, his father, Charles D. Berry, was principal of South Wabash School, which at the time included elementary and high school grades. Charles died of typhoid fever while taking additional training in education at Indiana University. His mother, Lillian, was left a widow when Loren was four years old and busied herself rearing the youngster, running a dressmaking shop, distributing samples of medicine door to door and working as a nurse in maternity and baby cases.

Berry showed an enterprise and imagination for salesmanship when he was quite young. As a boy of eight, he went door to door selling horseradish, which he dug from around Charley Creek, cleaned and ground himself. He sold it for five cents a glass. He used his mother's jelly glasses and then sold refills for the same amount. Later in grade school, he ran a small laundry route. First, he made collections on foot and then later bought a bicycle with a basket for pickup and delivery. He was able to make anywhere from five to forty cents on weekly collections and deliveries to twenty-five or thirty customers. He also had a newspaper route and sold the *Saturday Evening Post*. Berry has credited these early sales experiences with awakening an interest in selling that continued throughout his life.

He attended Wabash High School and while in high school turned to journalism and writing and earned three dollars per week reporting news for the *Wabash Plain Dealer*. He also ran a Gordon job press for the newspaper. Berry started Wabash High School's *Orange and Black* newspaper and was business manager for the school yearbook. Before he left high school, Berry sold vest pocket interurban timetables that carried advertising. He eventually sold timetables in most of the larger cities in the Midwest. He also sold space in the early days in such other advertising media as annunciators, used in barbershops, and in fire alarm cards.

Berry took a job in the Boston Store, Chicago, in the advertising department in 1908. Not making the financial progress there he expected, he returned to a reporting job on the Joliet, Illinois *Republican*. More interested in selling than in journalism, he went back to interurban timetables.

The turning point in his life came in 1909 when his brother-in-law, Ed Kneipple, invited him to sell advertising in the local telephone directory. He discovered that he could put out a directory and still enable the telephone company to make a certain amount of money on it. Success at Marion led to contracts at Kokomo and Logansport, handled on a published basis.

Berry went to Northwestern University for a while, and then in 1910 he and his wife went to Dayton, Ohio, where he set up his business under the name of the Ohio Guide Company, printing timetables. The extent of his wealth at that time was a few personal possessions and about $200 in cash. He decided to concentrate on the telephone directory business.

Under his guidance, the coast-to-coast telephone directory operation became one of the foremost telephone directory sales and publishing companies in the United States. Today, L.M. Berry and Company has contracts with five hundred independent and Bell Telephone companies in forty-one states and circulates publications in over nine thousand cities. It is now involved with international directory development, with international headquarters in Brussels, Belgium.

The Berry Company does not print the directories in which it sells space and compiles information. Berry's creed was "It can be done." He also said, "Our company has grown because I've had good people around me."

He described the Yellow Pages "as a running commentary on man's ability to move. Through the pages march the inventor with his inventions the manufacturer with his product and the professional man with his service—small businessman side by side with industrial giant."

In 1976, at the age of ninety-nine, Loren M. Berry was honored with the Horatio Alger Award during ceremonies at the Waldorf Astoria in New York City. He was one of fourteen persons to receive the medallion recognizing leading men and women who have, by their own efforts, pulled themselves up by their bootstraps in the American tradition and produced living proof that the "American Way" of achieving success still offers equal opportunity to all.

Among his many honors, Berry was Republican presidential elector (1972) for Ohio and was placed on the Telephone Hall of Fame Honor Roll by the Independent Telecommunications Pioneer Association. In 1982, his son, John, endowed the Loren M. Berry Chair on Economics at Dartmouth College in his honor. The Loren M. Berry Foundation was also established to oversee charitable gifts to the arts, education and medical research. Gifts have established the Loren M. Berry Center for Economic Education and the Ohio Stock Market Simulation at the University of Rio Grande.

Berry's son, John W., came into the business in 1946. By 1960, John had become the chairman of the board for the company, but Loren kept abreast of the progress of the business and was called upon for his competent advice, experience and recommendations. Loren M. Berry died on February 10, 1980, and is buried at Woodland Cemetery in Dayton, Ohio.

HOMER G. DAVISSON, PAINTER OF THE MISSISSINEWA

Homer G. Davisson, an Indiana impressionist painter, was born in Blountsville, Indiana, on April 14, 1866. He was a charter member of the Brown County Artist's Association. In 1888, a group of students in the city of Fort Wayne decided to form a class to work under the direction of some artist or recognized ability and training. The Art Association, as the group became known, was headquartered in the historic Hamilton mansion on Clinton Street.

Under the direction of their president, Mrs. Clark Fairbank, Davisson was hired as instructor of the art classes. He had studied at DePauw University and was later named one of its most distinguished alumni.

Impressed with the scenic beauty of the Mississinewa River, pictured here, Homer G. Davisson established a studio on its banks at Somerset.

This landscape was painted by Hoosier impressionist Homer G. Davisson, who summered in Wabash County.

He had also been a student at the Pennsylvania Academy of Fine Arts; Corcoran School of Art in Washington; and Art Students League of New York. He had also studied three years in landscape and portraiture under instructors in Europe. He spent two years at the Royal Bavarian Academy in Munich. The following year, he traveled and sketched on the continent and then brought the sketches back with him to Brooklyn, where he set about enlarging them.

While he was in Peru with an exhibit of watercolors, a group of public-spirited Fort Wayne citizens arranged a meeting with him in Huntington. They offered him a job as director of the Fort Wayne Art School. Davisson taught at the school from 1911 to 1947. According to art historian Mary Q. Burnet, he had "an almost divine gift for teaching." Pupils from the public school were given scholarships in the Saturday morning classes through Davisson's generosity, and adult students formed the day and evening classes. Public exhibitions were held from time to time.

His exhibits had wide variety and were seen in many places: Fort Wayne, Indianapolis, Marion, South Bend, Wabash and cities in Ohio, Pennsylvania and Illinois. His paintings were exhibited also in the Hoosier Salon both in

Chicago and Indianapolis, the Indiana Art Students League and the Fort Wayne Art School. For many years, his work was exhibited in the Radecki Art Gallery in South Bend.

In 1917, Davisson began making trips to Brown County and organizing European tours. In fact, he was in Switzerland with a tour during World War I. Fortunately, he spoke some French and he was able to get his group behind the French lines to London and aboard a ship for home.

His duties at the school often kept him from traveling south to Brown County and led him to seek out a nearby place to paint. He found his spot in old Somerset, Indiana, at the tail end of the Depression. His summer home and studio were located on West Main Street. Davisson also had a gallery in the IOOF Hall, above the former Dice Maisbury Drugstore. Impressed with the beauties of Somerset and the Mississinewa, he spent twenty-five years living and working there during the spring and summer months. During part of the summer, he conducted art classes in and around Somerset. Once or twice a week, it was not unusual to see his pupils painting around the studio.

His paintings became highly sought after in Wabash County because of their connection to scenes many people instantly recognize from their own backyards. The walls of many Wabash institutions, such as the Wabash Carnegie Public Library, Women's Clubhouse and Honeywell Center, have his paintings on display.

Considered a master of landscape, Davisson understood that nature had ever-changing lighting, shades and moods. Because of this deep knowledge, he refused to paint from memory, fearing that he would not capture the real feeling. Although he died on February 6, 1957, at the age of ninety-one, many local people still remember his studio and seeing him around old Somerset.

Davisson met his wife, Elizabeth, in 1924 in Brown County. He was painting and she was on a bus trip. Two years later, they met again in London, England. They honeymooned in France's Brittany, spent most of their married life in Fort Wayne and summered in the Somerset community. When she died in 1990, she left a collection of eighteen paintings to the Peabody Retirement Community in North Manchester. Another eight paintings pertaining to local history were given to Manchester College.

People

WABASH CARTOONIST DRAWS SWEENEY CHARACTER

Many citizens of Wabash put their lives on hold to support the war effort during World War II. Women left their homes to go to work in war-related industries. They sold their hair for the cross hairs in bomb sights and periscopes. Men left their careers to enter the service. Two men from Wabash entered and used their talents to tell the soldiers' story. They were Marvin P. Bradley and Roderick S. Hipskind. Bradley went on to draw *Speed Spaulding*, *Mary Worth* and *Rex Morgan, M.D.* Hipskind developed the GI Joe "Sweeney" character.

From the Seventh Army Front in France, 1945, the likable character "Sweeney" had gone to war! The humor depicted by Sweeney as a likable Irishman brought laughs from the Yanks of the United States VI Corps soldiers fighting on German soil. Sweeney was in the front line, in foxholes and on the Anzio beachhead. The character made light of the discomforts of war and peeves of the everyday duties the GIs had. As a cartoon character, he was a typical American GI, fighting the war with humor.

The cartoonist, Sergeant Roderick S. Hipskind—son of Mrs. J. Edward Hipskind, 107 Walnut Street, Wabash—served with the 636th Tank Destroyer Battalion. Hipskind served twenty-one months overseas, including training in North Africa and duty during the Salerno Invasion and the Battles of Mount Camino, Casino, Anzio, Rome and Plombino, Italy, as well as the invasion of southern France and the breakthrough north to the Rhine. According to a correspondent from the *Indianapolis Star*, Hipskind sketched battle scenes in watercolor, oils, charcoal, ink, pencil and "any art material I could find." He was also an amateur photographer.

Roderick Hipskind was probably known best to Indiana convention and club audiences as "Rodini, the Magican." He started his magic tricks while in high school and later appeared with professional troupes at conventions in Indianapolis, northern Indiana and in other places in the United States, as well as in shows in Europe.

Before entering the army on March 4, 1942, he was a commercial artist for Sears, Roebuck and the Beaudry Advertising Company of Florida. Hipskind studied art in Fort Wayne and was a pupil of landscape painter Homer G. Davisson for five years. Also, he was a member of little theatre groups and traveled in Florida with a professional stock company to perform his magic.

Roderick Hipskind made his GI Joe cartoons of "Sweeney" a front-line icon, a real treat for the fighting men of World War II.

Part IV

Places

———◆———

Lost Towns of Wabash

The names of towns and villages everywhere often reflect the names of the early settlers who immigrated to the area. Some names of towns have humorous origins. Many towns developed as roads and railroads became available. Such is the case in Wabash County.

Rose Hill: In 1872, the Cincinnati, Wabash and Michigan Railroad was built through the north edge of Pleasant Township, and a post office at Rose Hill was established. It was considered good for a growing center of trade due to the railroad. However, being close to Laketon and North Manchester did not allow for progress for this small town, which now has a cemetery, a church and a few other buildings that once made up the promising town.

Utica: On the north bank of the Wabash River, just within the Lagro Township line, the town of Utica was surveyed in 1837. It was located north of the Wabash and Erie Canal. Aside from the little grain warehouse, little existed, so the town plat of Utica was vacated by the county commissioners in 1853. It would become part of the plat of Belden.

Belden: A portion of the original site of Utica was afterward included in the hamlet of Belden, which was laid out by Elijah Hackleman in 1856. Its original proprietor was Archibald Kennedy. A post office was established in Belden in 1878; however, lack of growth caused the post office to be absorbed by rural mail service. It once had a gristmill and grocery store.

Bolivar: The town of Bolivar in Chester Township is associated with the Erie-Lackawanna Railroad in the early 1800s when it passed through Bolivar from Goshen to Anderson. The railroad crossed the Penn Central Big Four at Bolivar. And between Laketon and Bolivar there are rails in place looking down from State Road 13.

Choketown: There are two versions of the name Choketown, an area south of the Wabash River and south of Wabash as one goes toward the east. One version is that a man living near the area attempted to choke his wife to death. The other story is that at the Matlock Cemetery a horse and wagon broke loose, and the driver was choked to death by the reins as he was trying to stop the runaway team. Also known as Union Mills, it became a part of Wabash.

Majenica: This area was platted on December 16, 1842, but was promptly followed by New Holland on the twenty-third of the same month. It was laid out across the Salamonie River at the mouth of Deer Creek. It was originally named for Indian Chief Man-ji-ni-kia. New Holland, the location across the river, showed greater enterprise, thus the demise of Majenica.

New Harrisburg: This is an old village in Pleasant Township at the edge of Miami County that was laid out in 1856 by George Gearhart. According to records, William Carpenter built a small dwelling and store on the Wabash County side in 1858. Following that, more stores, a blacksmith shop, a wagon shop, some mills and several doctors occupied the town. In 1876, the post office at Niconza, three miles south in Miami County, was moved to the village, and in 1883, the Chicago and Atlantic Railroad grazed the southern edge, allowing for a depot. The community is also called Disko.

Puckerbrush: This town is supposedly named for a shrub or bush that when chewed would cause one to pucker. Early settlers in the 1880s opened a store and post office there and later named it Pioneer. The name "Pioneer" can be found painted on the side of the old blacksmith shop on Indian 124.

Monkeytown: At the corner of Pike Street extended and the Yankee Road in south Wabash, there was a small settlement centered on a tollbooth in the years 1890–1900. The road became a gravel road to Peru via the Mill Creek Pike. The name "Monkeytown" has an interesting story in that at one time a wagonload of monkeys was on its way to the circus grounds at Peru when a wheel fell off the wagon. There was a blacksmith shop nearby. The driver didn't have enough money to pay for wheel repairs, but he said he would put on a show of monkeys for payment of the wheel. This was agreed to, and after the show the area became forever known as Monkeytown.

Stockdale Mill, near present-day Stockdale, another lost town. The mills were important to the surrounding areas for the grinding of corn and wheat into flour.

The Roann Covered Bridge. At one time, Wabash County had five covered bridges; it now has two. This bridge, partially damaged by fire, was rebuilt.

America: Elihu Garrison and Jesse D. Scott platted the town of America; both had migrated to Wabash County in 1834. Garrison had been a soldier in the Black Hawk War. Scott was a clergyman. Both men settled in this bustling place on the road from Marion to Lagro. As many as one hundred teams passed through in a single day, headed to the canal and back, and the plank road made it easy for travel and overnight stays. Since the two men were complete opposites in politics and were rival candidates for judge, the name "America" seemed to stick as neutral. The town has long since disappeared, losing out to LaFontaine, but the cemetery is still there, and the America road still goes from Lagro to Marion.

Ashland: Platted in 1845 and settled by William Grant, who had settled two years before, the area was first called Grant's Land and also the Wolf Trap. Grant changed the name to Ashland for Henry Clay's home. Ashland was located on the west side of the boundary line of the Big Miami Reserve. In 1862, the town was incorporated as LaFontaine for Chief LaFontaine, leader of the Miami nation. Chief LaFontaine had become head of the tribe after the death of Richardville.

PROSPEROUS LIBERTY MILLS

Liberty Mills is a small community located on the east bank of the Eel River. It was platted by John Comstock and recorded on June 14, 1837. Two additions were later added to the community—one in April 1840 and another in March 1872. Early settlers of Liberty Mills were William Arnett, Daniel Baker, Charles L. Bates, Asa Beauchamp, Erastus Bingham, Hosea Bingham, Joseph Bloomer, Robert Casebolt, David Clapp, John Comstock, John W. Ellis, David Enyeart, Samuel Fages, Richard Helvey, A.W. Henley, C.V.N. Lent, Lewis J. Long, J.W. Nottingham, James Oakley, Samuel Pershing, John Rhodes, David Simonton, Jacob Simonton, John R. Simonton, Levi Smith, Daniel Swank, Henry Walker and John Whistler.

In its early days, Liberty Mills rivaled North Manchester as the major trading center in the northern portion of the county. This was due in part to the excellent plank roads leading into the town, which drew trade from Huntington and Kosciusko Counties.

Industry was another factor in its prosperity. At an early date, the town had a sawmill, a gristmill, a tannery and a very successful whiskey distillery. Grocery and dry goods stores, as well as saloons, lined the streets. The town's prosperity prompted John Comstock, who was active in local and state politics, to attempt on several occasions to create a new county, with Liberty Mills as its county seat. His hoped-for county would have been created out of surrounding counties.

Commonly known as Judge Comstock, the county histories have many interesting stories to tell of this man who came west from Lockport, New York. After a few years in Bristol, Ohio, he bought eighty acres west of Liberty Mills at a cost of about ten dollars per acre, arriving there in 1836 with his wife, six children and a hired man. In 1837, he erected a double-hewed log cabin and bought an additional forty acres, part of which he laid off into town lots. From then on, he engaged in various enterprises including a hog market, a sawmill, a gristmill, a tannery, a store, a woolen mill, a distillery and a detective agency. In 1858–59, he served as county representative to the state legislature and pioneered the improvement of cattle, bringing the first herd of shorthorns to Wabash County.

In 1839, he opened the first store in Liberty Mills, which he sold to Stitt & McCray in 1851. Other stores were opened by Erastus Bingham (1842), who also operated an ashery; John Whistler & Bro., merchant tailors (1843); Jacob Simonton & Company; Long & Abbott; and Whistler, Bender & Keagle. Joseph Bloomer, Wesley Parker, William Danner and Robert Carson also ran stores in the early days.

The first subscription school was established in Liberty Mills in the winter of 1838–39 and taught by Harriet Tullis in a cabin on Lot 39. A frame building was erected on Lot 51 in 1841. Later still, a two-story brick township-graded school was erected in 1872. Early principals of this school were John Myers, Professor McAlpin, A.E. Maurer, William Dover and William Shaffer. At the end of the 1958–59 school year, the school was closed, and the children of Liberty Mills were sent to North Manchester schools. The abandonment of the grade school, which is still standing, came about as a result of consolidation.

In early 1850, a plank road between Lagro and North Manchester was completed and had an important influence on the activities of Liberty Mills. The earliest bridge was built by private subscription and washed away in the flood of 1856–57. Other bridges were built to replace it. In 1973, a covered bridge similar to the North Manchester Bridge was built at a cost of $18.50 per lineal foot, or $3,339.20. The contract for the masonry was $8.59 per cubic yard, or $5,142.50. The bridge was 175 feet long. This bridge was sold at public auction on February 10, 1953, for $270.00 to Oscar Scott, Lloyd Capes, Norris Krom, Elmer Miller and Clinton Myers. The present bridge was completed in December 1954 at a cost of $67,214.78. The county commissioners have upgraded it several times since then.

During the Civil War, Liberty Mills furnished more soldiers for the Union army than any other town its size in the United States. There was one man who must receive credit for this role: George Abbott, the fighting parson of Liberty Mills.

Abbott was one of ten children born to James and Catharine (Tillman) Abbott, who in 1834 moved to the area. On July 26, 1838, he married Nancy Barrett and settled in Chester Township. Their first home was a simple log cabin with no windows and an animal hide hung over the opening for the door. To the family were born eight children. In 1842, he and his wife united with the Christian Church. By 1844, he began preaching and was ordained in 1849. In his first three years he made twenty-five cents. He was present at the organization of the Eel River Christian Conference and served in various capacities for fifty years. He was conference president in 1862, 1864 and 1869. Abbott was pastor for over twenty-five churches.

In the early 1860s, when the call came for troops, he went with the recruiting officers, helping to interest people. He was ever the warm friend to the soldier, and his eloquence led many to join the army. He would harangue the crowds that came to hear him, stating, "I will never ask any parent to do a thing that I am not willing to do myself." And with that, three of his sons enlisted, two never to return, making the supreme sacrifice for their country.

Throughout the war, George was a fearless worker for the Union. An incident was told of him that illustrates this nature. The body of a fallen soldier was returned home. The mother desired a funeral, but the Knights of the Golden Circle and other Southern sympathizers strong in the area declared that no funeral service should ever be preached there for a Union soldier. Preacher after preacher was asked, all refusing. Finally, the mother sent an appeal to Abbott. He accepted.

Going to the church building in which the funeral was to be held, he found it filled with people. In the back, he recognized some of the ringleaders of the sympathizers. As he opened his Bible on the pulpit, one of the fellows made a move as if to get up to leave the building. Before he got any further, Abbott drew two pistols from his pockets and, dropping his elbows on the

Bible, said, "I have been called here to preach this funeral, and I am going to do it. By power of the Almighty God I will shoot the first one who makes a move to leave this building until the service is ended." A gleam in his eye indicated that he meant what he said, and the funeral proceeded with pistols lying beside the Bible and a quiet and attentive audience.

After the Civil War, Liberty Mills continued to grow. It had one of the best bands in Indiana. Acey McFan was the leader, and three of his sons were also in the band. Band concerts were often given during the summer evenings. The bandstand was located downtown in the hopes of attracting business for merchants.

In 1873, Liberty Mills had three dry goods stores, one hardware store, two drugstores, two furniture stores, a hotel on the northeast corner of North Street and No. 2, two boot and shoe stores, two blacksmiths, one gristmill, one sawmill and three doctors: Banks, Lent and Lower. Continued growth seemed assured with the construction of the Detroit, Eel River and Illinois Railroad through the town. This led the town to become an important shipping point in the township for livestock and grain. However, the town lost its trading lead when the Big Four Railroad, running north and south, was built through North Manchester instead of Liberty Mills. Three disastrous fires also did not help. Trade and businesses began to slip away.

In 1882, businesses included C.T. Banks & Company dry goods, John Cordier's grocery, C.T. Banks & Company's flour mill, Nellie Martin's drugstore, Mrs. E.A. Banks's millinery, Dr. A.J. Carper, D.B. Long & John Johnson's blacksmith, Michael Cook's wagon smith, H. Wonderly's meat market and David Hartman's harness shop. The Chester Grange #1439 Patrons of Husbandry also had a meeting hall in a two-story brick building in town.

In 1894, business consisted of Reed & Abbott's meat market, W.A. Baugher's sawmill, Cordier & Welker's general store, Michael Cook's wagon shop, J.M. Fitch & Company's grocery and bakery, A.T. Hull's harness and agricultural implements, McFann's grocery, Martin & Robbins's blacksmith and S.B. Rittenhouse's manufacturer of seed sowers and adjustable wrenches. Daniel Mentzer was postmaster and also ran the hotel.

In 1898, the United States went to war with Spain. Members of the 159th Regiment from the North Manchester and Liberty Mills area were called up. One of the members distinguished himself not in fighting but in volunteering for the Walter Reed malaria experiment. His name was John R. Kissinger. He received the Congressional Medal of Honor for his sacrifice. He died in 1946 in Clearwater, Florida, and is buried in Huntington, Indiana.

In 1904, the No. 75 IOOF Lodge built a new lodge in Liberty Mills. In 1913, a fire, which started in the meat market of Matthew Ritter, did $15,000 worth of damage.

During the late nineteenth and early twentieth centuries, the Rittenhouse family became a prime mover in the community. Several industries were begun and operated by this family, including a flour mill that produced a fine grade of wheat flour known as Liberty Bird Flour and a factory that manufactured shovels. Nothing but ruins and memories remains of these industries today.

Another name that became important in Liberty Mills and Wabash County history was Arthur Coblentz. One of Coblentz's first glimpses of local fame was in 1927. He and Oscar Crabill were defendants in the very first Indiana lawsuit involving property damages caused by an airplane crash.

On June 29, 1927, Coblentz was in Oscar Crabill's airplane when they crashed into the home of Jenny Rader at Akron, Indiana. Rader sued for $1,000. Judge Kenner of the Huntington County Circuit Court dismissed the case for lack of evidence. Coblentz would go on to represent the county in the Indiana General Assembly.

On January 31, 1945, William Enyeart, ninety-eight, of Liberty Mills, passed away. He was the last Civil War veteran of the county.

In 1953, the following businesses were in Liberty Mills: Coblentz & Son garage run by Max and Arthur Coblentz, Frantz grocery run by Donald Frantz, Lee's Self Service run by Carl and Iva Heeter, Liberty Elevator managed by Glen Keaffaber, Liberty Mills Church of the Brethren, Liberty Mills EUB Church, Liberty Mills Sale Barn managed by Duane Garrison and Rittenhouse Seeder Factory run by Wayne Rittenhouse. There were 85 families living in the town with a population of approximately 266.

In 1968, the government, in an attempt to save money, closed the post office in Liberty Mills, which had been started in 1874. But through the efforts of the postmistress Iva Heeter, the government changed its mind. In 1970, the Heeters shut down their grocery store, and Iva continued as postmistress. In April 1979, the Liberty Mills Elevator was completely gutted by fire and not rebuilt. At the time, the town had 71 families and a population of 220 people.

History of Servia New Madison

Servia was first known as New Madison. The name was changed when the Erie Railroad went through in 1883. Since there was already a Madison, Indiana, it was thought that the name should be changed. Servia was platted by Peter Honius in 1856 with thirty lots in Section 22, Township 29, Range 7E. It was halfway between Lagro and Liberty Mills on the Lagro and Manchester road. Cross streets are Smith, Tanner, Sims and Bidwell.

Before the creation of the town, the area had the distinction of being the headquarters of the Witt gang that terrorized northern Indiana in the 1830s. Their headquarters were located on Pony Creek east of Servia. The gang was made up of horse thieves, counterfeiters, murderers and petty thieves. Witt, the leader, liked playing cards and gambling. He was known for his dissolute habits and would occasionally get drunk and raise quite a commotion. Miami Indians complained that their valuable horses were stolen by this gang. Witt disappeared from the area by 1840.

By 1875, there were seventeen buildings in town, including a schoolhouse, a post office (Christian Steller, postmaster), a grocery store and a steam sawmill. The sawmill was begun by Storey & Bowser and supplied the lumber for the North Manchester–Lagro plank road. Other owners were John Honius, Reed & West, David Wright and Honius & Company. The lumber was sawn from rough logs into pieces for wagon material, which was shipped to the Studebaker Bros. in South Bend. About 1900, the mill was moved to Jasper, Indiana.

After the canal, the railroad gave Servia impetus to grow and for many years was its principle source of income. Servia at one time was an important shipping depot for milk produced in the area. The Erie became the Erie-Lackawanna Railroad and later part of the ConRail system. It also brought to the community several grocery stores, blacksmith shops, a harness shop, a millinery, several saloons, an opera house and three hotels that took care of workers on the railroad and travelers. The last hotel was the Climax House, which burned down in the 1930s.

In the early hours of July 1, 1907, a fire broke out that threatened to engulf the community. It began in a blacksmith shop on Tanner and Main and spread north to Main Street proper. The town had no fire equipment, so the people of the community turned out with buckets to battle the blaze. At one point, more than a dozen buildings were on fire. George Emrick and Douglas Winesburg climbed to the roof of a brick business building next to the post office and doused embers that landed. Their efforts saved the post office and a nearby hotel from destruction. However, many businesses were destroyed and never rebuilt.

In 1911, Servia played a small role in U.S. history that would be reenacted seventy-five years later. In that year, a daredevil pilot named Cal Rodgers became the first man to fly an airplane across the United States. His airplane was the *Vin Fiz Flyer* and actually was a biplane purchased from the Wright brothers. He flew from Sheepshead Bay, New York, to Pasadena, California. This flight set the first major American aviation endurance and distance records and also was the first transcontinental flight. He landed sixty-nine times and had fifteen accidents.

At Huntington, Rodgers had wrecked his plane, avoiding a crowd of people. After having it fixed, he took off, following the Erie Railroad tracks. On October 6, 1911, twenty-one minutes after leaving, he passed over Servia, Laketon, Levings for a tower stop and then on through Disko. In 1986, on the seventy-fifth anniversary of the flight, Jim Lloyd of New York followed Rodgers's flight path in a replica of the *Vin Fiz Flyer*. On October 2, he was grounded because of weather and landed at the Servia Airport. Many citizens of Servia turned out to see the historic plane, and it was featured in local newspapers, as well. The airport was a grass field on the north edge of Servia.

In 1925, Servia began celebrating what were called the Servia Big Days. This became an annual homecoming celebration with all kinds of events. One competition that attracted a large amount of attention was the Liars Contest. Competitors came from neighboring states, as well as from all over Indiana, to participate. Many other contests called forth the talent of the residents of this small community. By the 1970s, this became the Servia Kids Days, with a parade, a potluck, a movie, contests, games and other entertainment.

In 1953, Servia had the following businesses: Bonnie's Grill and Barber Shop, Erie RR Passenger and Freight Station, Mutual Grain Company, Servia Christian Church, Servia School, the Village Store (run by R&M Barnhouse) and G.H. Walters & Sons Poultry. There were forty-seven buildings in the town, and it had a population of about 147.

The Servia of 1959 had an elevator, a general store, an egg and chicken market and a post office. The once active milk station closed in the 1950s, and the building was used for storage. Stanley Jordan spent a half-day at the depot.

On February 19, 1969, Servia was the scene of a serious train wreck. Fourteen freight cars derailed because of a broken wheel and piled up around the railroad station. One side of the train station was torn out.

Merchandise was strewn all along the tracks, including M16 rifle stocks, rifle tripods, basketballs, blenders and more. The county sheriff posted guards so that there would be no looting. The railroad station was declared a total loss and was torn down.

The general store closed about 1972. By 1976, Servia still had the elevator and fertilizer plant, a monument business and the post office. There were approximately eighty homes in the town. In 1979, the Servia Community Association began to make a park for the children of the community. Money was raised, and the park was laid out where the original log cabin school used to be located. Playground equipment was set up for the children to use.

About 1866, a group of disciples of Christ under Elder Bryant Fannin purchased a lot in Servia and built a substantial brick church. The original building had two entrances on the west side; the pulpit stood between them, facing east. Families funding its construction were Aughinbaugh, Foust, Hanley, Hevel, Hidy, Honius, Johnston, Kennedy, Krisher, Kuhle, Mowrer, Pauling, Shaubhut, Shock, Slusser, Steel, Steller, Voorhis, Walker and Young. It was named the New Madison Christian Church and later changed the name to Servia Christian Church. In 1931, it became the Servia United Church of Christ (Congregational Christian).

In 1931–32, the building was extensively remodeled. The front was changed to make one entrance, and the pulpit was moved to the east end of the room on a raised platform with a choir box. A new furnace, pews and floors were also added, as well as a balcony over the entrance. Sunday school rooms and a kitchen were also added. In 1959–60, the present entrance, vestibule, classrooms and a fellowship hall were constructed. A parsonage was built to the south of the church in 1965. By 1975, the church had a membership of two hundred.

The first school in the area was a log cabin school constructed in 1857. It was located where the town park is today. In 1886, a two-story brick building was built. By 1899, it had nine grades with one hundred students and teachers. This building was replaced in 1914 on the same site and used until 1957. The school was discontinued with the consolidation of the Chester-Manchester schools and later torn down.

How Silver Creek Got Its Name

In 1826, the Miami Indians gathered at a large spring that ran into the Wabash River. That spring, now known as Paradise Spring, is located in the city of Wabash. It was the site of a treaty with representatives of the U.S. government. The treaty opened up northern Indiana to white settlement. Part of the treaty allowed for a payment, an annuity, to be made yearly to the tribes in return for their land.

Annuity payments were generally given to the chief of the tribe and distributed by him to the rest. For many years, annuity payments were made to Chief Richardville, who lived at the "Forks of the Wabash" near Flint Springs, present-day Huntington.

The Indian agent at this time lived at Logansport. There was only one road leading from Logansport to the Forks. Originally an Indian trail, by act of the state legislature it had been widened and somewhat improved in 1828—yet it was only forty feet wide. It was over this road that the annuity payment had to pass through Wabash County.

The annuity payment, in those days, was made in silver coins. The money was carried in strongboxes. Indian traders would follow so that they could separate the Indian from his silver as quickly as possible. This was done by selling goods or alcohol, generally the latter. Some of these hangers-on were shifty characters, so an armed guard was necessary.

Sometime in the early 1830s, an attempt to steal the silver was made. A trader by the name of Ferguson had been following the party of officials headed to the Forks. The party had reached a small creek by noon. They stopped for lunch and left the money unguarded. For Ferguson, this was too much temptation. Seeing his chance, he seized one of the boxes full of money. As the box was heavy, he secreted it in the nearby creek and covered it with a large flat stone in the hopes of returning later to recover it.

However, the box was soon missed by the party. Suspicion fell on Ferguson. He denied that he had taken the money and swore that he knew nothing of it. His denials only incensed the men, as they were liable for the money. He was threatened with physical harm if he did not tell where he put it. Several men got out a rope and threw it over a tree. A noose was made. The rope was put around his neck, and he was hanged but was cut down before his life was extinguished. This process was repeated a number of times until he made a confession. He described the location of the stolen money, and it was recovered.

The party officials informed Ferguson that they would spare his life and let him go on the condition that he never again be seen in the neighborhood.

Ever since this incident, the creek that is located in northeastern Lagro Township has been known as Silver Creek. And every so often, people are seen walking up Silver Creek looking for silver coins. After all, according to legend, not all the silver was found.

Part V

Business and Industry

First Industry in Wabash County

The Indian Mill, built on Mill Creek just south and east of Richvalley, was constructed in 1820 by the U.S. government according to a provision of the 1818 Treaty of St. Mary's. It was to be located within a nine-hundred-square-mile reserve set aside for the Miami Indians. The second clause of the treaty provided for the government to build both a gristmill and a sawmill at a site to be chosen by chiefs of the tribe. It further provided that a blacksmith and a gunsmith would be located at the site as well.

The Miami Indian mill was built on Mill Creek in 1820 by Benjamin Level at a cost of $3,600. Lewis Davis was appointed as the first miller and continued in that capacity for six years at a salary of $350 to $500 per year. He moved to the site, which was very isolated (his closest neighbors were at Lafayette and Fort Wayne). However, there were many visitors to the area besides Indians, as it was on the main trail connecting the two communities.

In 1821, the mill was visited by Henry R. Schoolcraft so he could inspect the works and report on its condition. He found the mill "seated on a copious brook in a small valley, buried by the surrounding forest growth." He found no signs of Davis "nor any traces of the mill having been recently visited, or put into motion." The mill appeared to be in sound condition and well constructed. The dam, however, had been breached. At least $150 was expended to repair the dam, which was fixed by October 1824.

In July 1826, Gillis McBean was appointed to replace Davis, who had operated the mill for two years. Just before the arrival of McBean, Hugh B. McKeen visited the site and found both the mill and dwelling house to be "the abode of serpents and retreat of toads." The mill in particular "was the rendezvous for otters and raccoons. The saw is broken." In June 1827, Reeve Chapman repaired the running gears of the sawmill McKeen had found broken and also put new cogs in the wheel of the gristmill at a cost of $1,015.21.

McBean found the area too isolated and by June 1828 had spread the word that he was leaving. Many began to approach General Tipton, the Indian agent, for the position. Tipton knew Jonathan Keller from when he lived in Harrison County, Indiana, and was responsible for bringing him and his family to Wabash County. Jonathan Keller came to the Miami Indian mills on September 28, 1828. He was employed in this position for the next two years, at which time it was decided that the mill was no longer necessary. He joined Robert Wilson, who had arrived the previous year to operate the blacksmith shop.

Jonathan Keller brought his wife and eight children along with Sumer Boone, a cousin of Daniel Boone. Jonathan Keller's youngest child, Jonathan Jr., was the first white child born in what is now Wabash County, on May 8, 1830. On October 3, 1832, Keller purchased the east half of the northeast quarter of Section 14, Township 27, Range 5E, as well as other property. Keller wrote back to family that he had left in Harrison County, telling them of the land and opportunities here. His brothers, James and Anthony, moved to join him and settled in the same area. This locality was known in early days as the "Keller Settlement," later "Keller's Station" and now as Richvalley.

Keller's oldest child, Elizabeth, was married to another pioneer of the county, Joseph McClure, in 1832 near Richvalley, becoming the first white couple to be married in what is now Wabash County, although at the time the land was part of Cass County.

Jonathan stayed in the county and eventually became an associate judge of Wabash County. He also at one time ran a hotel in Huntington County. Many of the Keller family can be found buried at the Richvalley cemetery. In the small community of Richvalley, in front of the Lion's Clubhouse, you can find one of the original millstones from the old Miami Indian Mills, the first industry in the county.

—›·‹—

SOUTH WABASH RURAL HOME CURE

During the 1840s, the "cold water cure," or hydropathy as it was also called, created quite a stir among those in the medical profession. It threatened to replace the barber pole and the practices of bloodletting and using leeches. The water cure taught the health-giving effects of pure water when taken internally or externally. The practitioners of this method committed heresy when they claimed that patients should conserve their blood instead of giving it up. This cure also encouraged people to watch their diet, bathe frequently, wear loose-fitting clothing and properly ventilate their homes.

Of course, Wabash people knew better. They could eat what they liked—the greasier the better. Everyone knew of vapors, that the night air could kill you and that bathing would shorten your life. In fact, the barber, Dan Ferguson, was the first to introduce the bathtub to Wabash when he had one installed in 1878.

As for clothing, well, the height of fashion required everyone to wear red flannel. Women had to wear two or three petticoats—one to be quilted—dress skirts that dragged on the ground, bustles to carry the weight and hoops to keep the dress from impeding their walk. Heavy corsets (stays) kept their forms upright. Men, not to be outdone, wore collars as stiff as boards almost to their ears and wrapped silk cloths around their necks to keep them up and tight.

By 1859, hydropathy had finally made it to Wabash via two upstart doctors on the south side of the river. One was Dr. David Miles and the other Dr. Stephen Jones. Miles ran a bath out of his brick home on the north side of Pike Street. Jones, who had practiced medicine for twelve years and had run the water cure at Granville, Ohio, lived on what is now Vernon Street. In August, both doctors formed a partnership and built a water cure on the northwest corner of Pike and Vernon Streets. By June 1862, the public was informed that the rural home water cure was open for business and would provide every means to "improve the health and physical condition of those placed in their care." Besides Miles and Jones, three other doctors joined them: Uriah T. Woodbury, Mary Bryant and Dr. Alexander.

The main building was three stories high in the front and four in the back, with twenty-seven rooms. Wide balconies extended the entire length of each story. The basement had a dining room, a kitchen, a washroom and a cellar with a large spring and an engine and boiler for hoisting water. There was also an office, a parlor, a large reception room, twenty-five double and single sleeping rooms and an attic with two large dormitories. There were also two cottages, an icehouse, a barn and a gymnasium on the property.

They employed the "Swedish movement cure," a system that believed that the nutrition and development of any organ or organs occurred in direct relation with the amount and quality of exercise and nutrition. This movement was the brainchild of Peter Henrick Ling of Sweden.

The doctors provided special equipment by which one could exercise any and all muscles. They had apparatus for straightening hunchback, round shoulders and crooked spines, strengthening abdominal muscles and muscles of the side, back and limbs and for increasing the size of one's chest or waist. One patient said, "We are rolled, tousled, stretched and clapped into a state of health."

In the spring of 1865, Melissa James of Lincolnville took sick and was sent to take the cure. She had a severe cold in her throat and lungs. While she was there, the water cure had at least sixty other patients. She was charged nine dollars per week. Her treatment consisted of being covered with two towels wet with cold water, and red flannel was wrapped around her neck and chest. Wet towels covered her whole body at night. She was given a hot foot bath for thirty minutes and then dipped in cold water and rubbed dry. She was then put in a very warm bed.

At 6:00 a.m., a nurse dressed her and sent her out to walk as far as she could before breakfast. Melissa went only two blocks. At the end of nineteen weeks, she could walk three miles and back before breakfast. After breakfast, her daily routine involved going to the gymnasium at 9:30 a.m. for all kinds of exercise, followed by a bath and an hour-long nap. Everyone then went for a walk until 3:00 p.m., when dinner was served. After dinner, everyone went to the parlor for a social hour.

Ida Woodbury, the daughter of Dr. Woodbury, later recalled much of the life at the water cure. She would always compare it to a Turkish bath with steam room showers and tubs of all sizes. One of her most vivid memories was that all women, patients, nurses and help had to wear the bloomer dress. Also, the diet loomed large in her thoughts. All patients primarily enjoyed a vegetarian diet, made up of vegetables and fruits grown on-site. Small portions of roasted and boiled meats, except for pork, were served.

Pickles, catsup, mustard, pepper and even salt were discouraged, as they were thought to impair the natural appetite and appreciation of the natural flavor of foods. Graham crackers and cracked wheat, well boiled with plenty of milk and cream, were encouraged for breakfast. No greasy foods were served, nor were rich desserts.

Recreation was a large part of the curative process. In the large parlors were books, magazines and quiet games, such as checkers, dominoes, Parcheesi and more. Once a week, dances were held in the dining room. Bloomer dresses were then discarded for evening wear.

The doctors also published the *Western Health Journal* at a cost of eight dollars for twenty issues. The journal dealt with methods of preserving one's health. By 1966, the water cure was just a memory. Why it closed seems to be a mystery not yet solved. The building and grounds, though, became the Female Academy, the County Orphanage and, finally, the South Side Fire Station.

INDUSTRIES PUT WABASH ON THE MAP

When immigrants came to Wabash County, they brought with them the basic needs for survival. Before long, they found that other great needs were desired, so they had to use their own initiative and labor to devise products to make living easier. Whether it was a tool of various sorts, a cradle, a broom, utensils or furniture, they used their own labor to make them. Indeed, "necessity is the mother of invention."

Craftsmen became important individuals to supply some of these needs. Blacksmiths and harness makers developed their trades. In 1847, Arthur Kennedy became one of Wabash's first harness makers. Carpenters were in great demand to construct better homes than log cabins. Also in 1847, William Andres received a patent for a windmill and wind works. There was a definite need for supplying water for family and farm use. And in the same year, coffin makers Oliver Hill and Hiram Stearly produced coffins for the deceased.

By 1848, a list of industrialists in Wabash showed an ironworks for Madison Whiteside; stoves and tinware by L. O'Brien and John Davis;

The Big Four railroad depot near the "cut" on East Market Street. It was first located at Canal and Huntington Streets.

cabinetmakers John McKelsey, Hiram Clary and Oliver Hill; and wagon and carriages made by William Luark. In 1848, tailors included Ben Pawling and Tim Craft. Before these two, Andy Lowman was listed as Wabash's first tailor, lasting forty years. The first shoemaker was William Iliff.

In 1849, T.F. Payne was in the furniture-making business. According to a September 1850 newspaper, Wabash had three hardware stores, some iron and stove stores, four blacksmiths, five cabinet shops, a foundry, flour mills and several warehouses.

Industry in Wabash, however, may have been affected in 1850, as at least nine individuals left for the gold rush: S.A. Busick, Joseph Busick, M.H. Baker, Marcus King, A.P. Burr, Joshua Reeves, Thomas Roberts, U.N. Pumphrey and William Walker. However, by 1854 William Whiteside had a furniture-undertaker business, Fowler and Donaldson were clock makers, W. Burgett was a gunsmith, M.I. Thomas and James Stoops were saddle and harness makers and William Launder, Jesse Morgan and George Hoover were blacksmiths.

There were woolen mills, the first started in 1855 by Robert Cissna, and sawmills courtesy of Mark Jones and Hugh Hanna. Water power from the canal was used to power some sawmills. The first planning mill was started in 1852 by Levi Dollison. Silversmiths Catlin, Sackett, Mayer, French and

Diehl's Manufacturing Company, established in Wabash in 1909 and still in business today.

Sandoz, who was also an optician and jeweler, were in business by the 1860s and 1870s. There were even two cigar factories listed in 1889.

By the turn of the century or a few years prior, numerous businesses and industries had begun operations. B. Walter Company began operations in 1887 and still continues to make table slides to the present day. F.J. Rettig & Sons in 1900 built a machine shop for all kinds of machine work. In 1897, a firm known as the Wabash Canning Company (began as the Great Western Canning Company) canned seasonal produce such as corn, tomatoes, beans, pumpkins and sauerkraut. In 1895, the Wabash Baking Powder Company was organized with Roy Ryan and W.M. Gamble as officers. The company manufactured baking powder, as well as soda, cornstarch, extract, powdered skim milk and cocoa.

The 1897–98 Wabash Directory lists a Screen Door Company, with J.A. Bruner as president, manufacturing pine and hardware screen doors and the "Wabash" adjustable window screen. Also listed was the Wabash Soap Company manufacturing the "best grade of soap."

G.M. Diehl Works first started in Peru in 1908 and moved to Wabash in 1909, making industrial machinery. The Cardinal Cabinet Company (later to become the Wabash Cabinet Company) was known for its new "Mother

Hubbard" cupboard in 1900. Yarnelle Lumber Company supplied the needs of Wabash in the early days and still does today. Originally, it received lumber goods from the canalboats. The Wabash School Furniture Company was started before the turn of the century by William Henley, D.W. Lumaree and John Ross, as schools were now a necessity for the community. Other firms, like the United Paper Board Company (long known as the Coating Mill), had been a part of the Wabash Paper Company branch and the United Boxboard and Paper Company. They were in business by 1898, and the Diamond Match Company was another business that existed at the same time.

The Honeywell Heating Specialty Company in 1905 produced a system of hot water heating. In 1901, the company had received a patent for this system. Later, the firm merged and became the Minneapolis-Honeywell Company and still later was the MarkHon firm in Wabash.

Ford Meter Box Company manufactured meter settings and water meters. It began in Wabash in 1898 in the basement of the Diehl's factory, with Edwin H. Ford as president. Another company, the United States Button Company, formerly of Muscatine, Iowa, manufactured pearl buttons from shells taken from the Wabash River. Samuel Bowlby started the firm here.

One of the important firms to appear in Wabash was that of the Service Motor Truck, started in 1911, with Fred Walters as president. It kept Wabash busy from 1911 to 1921 producing trucks of various capacities. It furnished the government with military trucks, oil and logging trucks and huckster wagons, and prices were listed from $1,400 up. Trucks were sent to other parts of the country for various uses. Its history reports that the firm began with one truck made by three persons, but with advanced techniques it soon had an assembly line with as many as 750 employees at one time. The firm also made railway cars. In 1926, the firm was bought by Relay Motors; still later in 1936, General Tire and Rubber took over the building.

There have been other companies serving the Wabash community during the twentieth century. A Pioneer Hat Works in 1901, with Nathan Meyer as owner, made hats for Wabash. There was a glove factory, a toy block company and a novelty wood works, and earlier in 1873 a water bicycle was built and used on the canal by William G. Thompson.

In 1918–19, Motox Tractor Company began making tractors for agricultural use on Manchester Avenue. It became more or less a sales agency but did produce one tractor. In 1919, the Service Motor Truck firm

The Big Four railroad yards were important to the growth of business and industry in Wabash. Today, only one building remains of this complex to remind us of our railroad past.

got in the business of building the Sattco airplane. The airplane industry in Wabash more or less transformed into a training center. About the same time, in 1908–10 in North Manchester, DeWitt Automobile was started. The F.J. Rettig firm on the south side also made an automobile in 1907 as an experiment in the firm's garage. Seven were known to have been made. The automobile made the same impact on Wabash as on the rest of the world in the early 1900s.

Over the years, some industries have existed in Wabash for short periods of time. Some like Deluxe Coils made electrical components; Wall-Away made custom storage and shelving. Some were used in local schools. Downs and Wiles produced concrete products. A.F. Billings provided decorations. Celotex was a rock wool firm. Spencer Cardinal, before selling in 1953, made furniture. Temple Industries was in the steel fabrication business. The Weitzel Display Case Company made counter display cases in 1930. Vice Brothers started in 1940 making wood and metal castings and did pattern and foundry work. General Electric made

TV cabinets. Eagle Picher worked with mineral wool insulation. Hipsher Tool and Die is still in business.

General Tire and Rubber became an important factory in Wabash, starting in 1936; the firm had bought the Service Motor Truck Company building. It made rubber products used in various ways and was one of Wabash's largest employers at that time.

During World War II, many of the factories in Wabash made useful items for the government. Their products helped the war effort in many ways.

Other smaller companies in the county from time to time have served Wabash residents. The advent of improved transportation by rail and automobile has changed the way factories and businesses have operated. Now, with the technology of the twenty-first century, tremendous changes have occurred, not just in Wabash County but in the rest of the world, too. Wabash is no longer an isolated area in industry, and the early immigrants would be amazed at the changes in lifestyles. Progress in all manner is part of the present-day world.

WABASH SCREEN DOOR COMPANY

In 1894, the Wabash Novelty Wood Works was organized by Henry M. Gardner and James Meyers. Their factory was located on Comstock Street. It produced baluster, counters, brackets, moldings, toy wagons, sleds and the "Wabash" screen door.

Novelties in wood soon became a secondary line and were pushed out entirely in 1887 because of the increased demand for the celebrated "Wabash" screen door. On September 2, 1890, the name of the company was changed to the Wabash Screen Door Company, giving birth to an industry that became a leader in the United States. The company had its offices located at the corner of Wabash and Water Streets. The mill, warehouse and yards occupied a full square bounded by Wabash, Water and Mimi Streets. The mill and warehouse occupied eighty-one thousand square feet of floor space.

In September 1891, the company established a branch in Rhinelander, Wisconsin. After a fire destroyed the Rhinelander plant in 1901, it was moved to Minneapolis, Minnesota. Another plant was established in Memphis, Tennessee, in the same year.

On August 18, 1897, Edward M. Kemp and Harvey W. Weesner purchased from the Wabash interests three-fourths of the outstanding capital stock. With this move, the company left Wabash, yet the name was kept the same. By 1900, other businesses were to be found in the building. The south wing of the factory was occupied by the Mexican Art Leather Company. In 1907, Kothe, Wells and Bauer occupied the building on Miami and Cass Streets.

From small beginnings, this company became a national concern, whose buildings can still be found bearing the name Wabash Screen Door Company.

<hr />

THE BUTTON FACTORY IN WABASH

Not much thought is given to those small items that are used to fasten clothes together, but those small items, buttons, were and still are one of our most commonly used household items. And many were made right here in Wabash.

In 1912, Mr. Sam Bowlby, an agent of the United States Button Company of Muscatine, Iowa, came to Wabash and established a factory, making buttons from mussel shells found in the Wabash River.

The Wabash River was full of mussels of all types. In 1988, a study revealed a bed of fan shell mussels living around the Carroll Street Bridge. This bed was not very wide, approximately ten yards across, but it was possibly very long. Fan shell mussels are similar to clam shells and are about three inches across, with a pearly white interior. It takes up to 15 years to reach maturity, and they can live up to 150 years. Wabash has between thirty and thirty-five species of mussels, yet at one time there were seventy known species.

Mussel fishing had been established in Iowa as far back as 1891, when a button cutter factory produced buttons from freshwater mussel shells.

From Iowa to Indiana, camps of musselers became common in streams of Indiana. This industry became a way of life that proved popular, especially when mussel shells were found to contain pearls, causing a great deal of excitement.

According to Wabash descendants of Mr. Bowlby, he had started working in a button factory in Muscatine, Iowa, when he was twelve years old. He had worked his way up from being a button cutter to manager before coming to Wabash.

Indiana mussels provided the highest quality for pearl culture, and for approximately twenty years, mussel shells supplied numerous button factories with shells. The Ohio, Wabash and White Rivers and upper Mississippi rivers produced the source of mussel shells for the cultured pearl industry. The rivers were dragged for the mussels, and the shells, called "blanks," were cut with round saws. The buttons were sent to Muscatine for polishing and finishing and then sorted and hand-sewn on cards ready for the market. Button cutting usually occurred during winter months. Shells not used were sometimes ground up for chicken feed and even used for driveways.

An article in *Outdoor Indiana* from May 1982 gave the history of dragging for mussel shells in the Wabash River. When first operating the business, the mussel boat mules would drag downstream, as the mussels were located in gravel beds, waiting for hooks to grab them. After taking his catch, the musseler would carry it to the factory, often using horse and wagon. At some camps along the river, the shells would be carried to the railroad, where they were loaded in boxcars and sent on their way. The musseler's day began at sunup, and as he poled downstream to fill his boat, he worked hard. After taking the catch, the mussels were steamed open, and the search for pearls began. Slugs were imperfect pearls, which were also sold. Only one pearl in as many as fifty had much value. Although it was a lucrative business and exciting at times, it was hard work. As many as fifty people were employed at the factory at one time.

Pearls are formed in mollusks, such as mussels and oysters, when a foreign body such as a grain of sand enters the shell. The seed is coated by a secretion produced by the mussel. The value of the pearl depends not so much on size but on color, luster and shape.

By 1925, the supply of mussel shells in the Wabash River was becoming exhausted, and the plant was closed. Mussel shells are highly sensitive to pollution, which resulted in the threat of decreased growth of mussel shells. On June 3, 1930, the State Department of Conservation placed a five-year ban on mussel hunting and removal of mussels from the Eel River, but at that time no others in Wabash County were included. During the time of the ban, sections of the rivers would be used as mussel breeding grounds.

In 1925, Warren F. Spiker bought the old U.S. Button Factory on 592 South Wabash Street. This ended the button industry in Wabash.

About the Authors

One of seven children, Gladys Dove was born on a farm in Daviess County, Indiana. Receiving a county scholarship, she attended and graduated from Indiana State Teachers College. During World War II, she served as a civil service librarian at NAS Corpus Christi and NAS Chase Field. After the war, she obtained a master's degree at Indiana University. She then taught in LaPorte County and West Lafayette. She became the Wabash High School librarian, a position she held for forty years.

For a brief time, she served as interim librarian at the Wabash Carnegie Public Library and taught English at Ivy Tech College in Wabash.

After the death of her husband, Garl C. Harvey, she traveled to various countries, and she is interested in genealogical and historical research.

Ron Woodward was born and raised in New Albany, Indiana. He graduated from Indiana University while serving in the United States Navy. After his discharge, he received his master's degree from Ball State University. He has taught in the Greater Clark County school system, Muncie school system and Wabash City Schools. He has also taught at the Upper Wabash Vocational School and a methods class at Manchester College. He has served as president of the Wabash County Historical Society and Wabash County Genealogical Society, which he helped to form.

He has been honored as Indiana Geography Teacher of the Year, Wal-Mart Teacher of the Year, 2000 Hoosier Historian from the Indiana Historical Society and Semifinalist Teacher of the Year. He has served as Wabash County historian since 1981 and was a sponsor of the Indiana Junior Historical Society Club for twenty-five years.

Visit us at
www.historypress.net